COLD BLOODED
EVIL

COLD BLOODED
EVIL

The true story of the 'Ipswich stranglings'

NEIL ROOT

JOHN BLAKE

Published by John Blake Publishing Ltd,
3 Bramber Court, 2 Bramber Road,
London W14 9PB, England

www.blake.co.uk

First published in hardback in 2008

ISBN: 978 1 84454 481 3

British Library Cataloguing-in-Publication Data:

A catalogue record for this book is available from the British Library.

Design by www.envydesign.co.uk

Printed in Great Britain by CPI Bookmarque, Croydon, CRO 4TD

3 5 7 9 10 8 6 4 2

Papers used by John Blake Publishing are natural, recyclable products
made from wood grown in sustainable forests. The manufacturing
processes conform to the environmental regulations of the country
of origin.

Every attempt has been made to contact the relevant copyright-holders,
but some were unobtainable. We would be grateful if the appropriate
people could contact us.

CONTENTS

MAP SHOWING THE LOCATION OF WHERE THE FIVE BODIES WERE FOUND

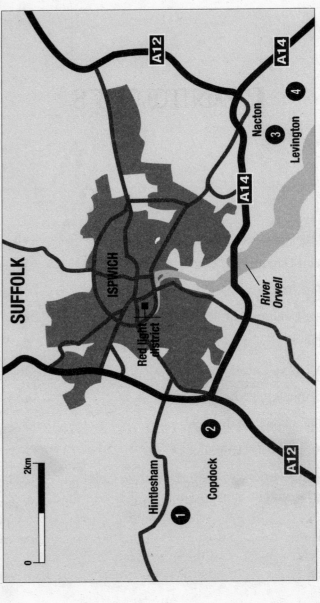

1. Gemma Adams, aged 25.
2. Tania Nicol, aged 19.
3. Anneli Alderton, aged 24.
4. Annette Nicholls, aged 29, and Paula Clennell, aged 24.

PROLOGUE

In early December 2006 most people were winding down, mentally preparing for the relaxed limbo-land that the average British Christmas brings. The decorations were coming down from the attic and being dusted off, the Christmas lights checked, cards written and sent, and office parties planned. It was the usual drill in the run-up to the festive period, a time to relax and catch up with friends and family.

The town of Ipswich in Suffolk was no different from anywhere else. The town itself and the sleepy villages surrounding it had no idea that their pleasant repose was about to be shattered. There was no sense that this Christmas would be different to any other. But the events of the following weeks would unfold at a ferocious pace and the people of the area would never see life in the same way again. Sinister events of this magnitude can only cast a shadow on the psyche of a community.

The media storm that blew up would gather pace until

it was a terrifying whirlwind – local, then national and finally international coverage. From brief mentions to headlines, and then to blanket coverage. There was to be no escape for the people of Ipswich and no release for the British nation as a whole, as every day brought new revelations, suspicions and finally arrests.

George Orwell once wrote that the reason we like to read about murder is because it feels so removed from us. We can sit in our cosy living rooms, letting family life continue. It only happens to other people. Unless we are directly connected to a homicide victim, we can indulge our morbid curiosity and 'safe' fear with little emotional investment. Perhaps we feel a slight shiver as we draw the curtains, thankful that we are comfortable in our homes, tucked up in warm beds. We feel sympathy and compassion, but the lack of any real impingement on our daily lives allows us to sleep well. Especially if the murder victim seems to have lived in a very different world from our own.

But it was not like that for the families of five young women in Ipswich and the surrounding area that winter. The women in question may have worked as prostitutes and lived a life most of us know only from newspapers, books and films. They may have had different experiences. But no one should judge them. They too were human beings with feelings and aspirations that were probably very little different from our own.

The shockwaves will go through that part of Suffolk for years, with Ipswich and the villages around it forever changed, if not scarred by these terrible crimes. The evil of these actions is hard to understand and explain. On one hand these are extreme and thankfully rare events, yet on the other hand we may be reminded of the writer Hannah

Arendt's famous quotation about 'the banality of evil'. Horrors might be difficult to comprehend but try to understand them we must. This is the story of the Ipswich stranglings.

CHAPTER ONE

THE DAWNING OF DISBELIEF

SATURDAY, 2 DECEMBER 2006
THORPES HILL, HINTLESHAM, SUFFOLK
11:50am

The Suffolk landscape in winter can be very beautiful, the falling leaves gently rustled by the wind a reminder of time passing and the inevitability of the life cycle. The bare branches of centuries-old trees stand in haunting silhouette against the white sky. This is the real English countryside, where the rustic majesty of the fields is richly veined by meandering brooks and streams. In such a tranquil setting it is easy to forget about the essential violence of nature.

The small village of Hintlesham is to be found about 7 miles (11.3km) to the west of the town of Ipswich. Although clustered around a main road, this is a quaint and simple place where little changes, and when it does, much comment is aroused. On an ideal summer's day, parts of it can be chocolate-box perfect. Not the obvious place for a macabre discovery.

Trevor Saunders was doing his regular round of inspection that morning around the Thorpes Hill area. Employed by Hintlesham Fisheries, he knows every metre of his stretch. Mr Saunders would later say:

'I was doing my normal patrol along Burstall Brook to check on any blockages when I noticed two round, smooth surfaces sticking out of the water, which I later found was the woman's bottom. Initially I thought it was a dummy. I went into the brook to make sure and, on further investigation, found it was a body. It was face down, under water. I had to move a little bit of debris to make sure it was a body. Then I phoned the police.'

The tranquillity of the scene was soon shattered as the police closed off the crime scene and surrounding area and conducted the usual thorough forensic examinations and photographs before the body was taken away.

The next day Suffolk Police made a statement confirming the identity of the body. She was Gemma Adams and she had lived at Blenheim Road, Ipswich, just on the outskirts of the town centre itself. She had been reported missing by her partner over two weeks earlier on Wednesday 15 November, when she failed to return home in the early hours of the morning. Gemma had worked as a prostitute, primarily to fund a serious drug habit. On the night of her disappearance she had gone to work on the streets of Ipswich's red light district.

A police spokeswoman confirmed that the death was being treated as 'suspicious' and that the post-mortem had not established any definite cause of death.

Appeals for information started immediately. The police knew very well that the first 48 hours after the discovery of a crime are crucial – any witness statements, crime scene evidence and possible leads would be fresh. As Gemma's body had been stripped before being left in the water, the police knew how urgent it was to find her clothing and other effects. Developments would soon be forthcoming on this front, but few strong leads to the possible offender.

It was a shocking day. Suffolk does not have a high crime rate, despite having had some high-profile cases over the years. These were exceptions, not the norm. In a 2004 Suffolk Police survey, 45 per cent of Suffolk residents questioned felt safe where they lived and only 17 per cent were worried about violent crime (Source: *Suffolk First,* June, 2004). Compared with similar surveys carried out in other parts of the country, these figures are good.

But murder can occur at any time and in any place. Human nature does not take geography into account when entering dark recesses of the mind. General trends can be followed, with urban, more deprived areas more likely to experience violent crime. Although murders can almost always be profiled geographically, the mind of a killer is as random as any mind, especially if there is a sexual motive.

The finding of Gemma Adams made the front page of the Ipswich *Evening Star*. While shocking and saddening to the community, it could have been an isolated prostitute murder, a phenomenon we will discuss later. But there was no getting away from the callousness shown in the way Gemma Adams was dumped. The lack of respect and compassion, the indignity of being left naked, lying face down, in little more than a ditch. What kind of evil could be behind this?

Unfortunately, it was only the beginning.

Surrounded by sleepy villages and traditional agricultural land, Ipswich is the county town of Suffolk, with a population of 140,000 people in 2006. Looking like many a provincial British town of the twenty-first century, with the predictable chain stores and shops, gradually losing individual identity as the years pass, it is now an expanding commercial centre. Yet there are still many historical points of interest, even if it lacks the excitement and glamour of a major city or the magnetism of a cathedral city.

Founded at the tip of the Orwell estuary, the site on which Ipswich stands has been inhabited since the Stone Age. Like many other places, the river that runs through it was always an important trade route. The River Orwell is also well known for giving a young aspiring writer named Eric Blair his new name in the early twentieth century. He would of course become the internationally respected author George Orwell.

During the seventh, eighth and ninth centuries the town was known as Gippeswic. It was actually the first and most famous Anglo-Saxon port and one of the most important trading communities in the country.

There are many surviving traces of the medieval period in the town, from the layout of the streets to a number of historic churches from that time. The major industry of the town in this period was the very lucrative trade in Suffolk cloth, but this market went into sharp decline as England moved into the Georgian period, and this lack of prosperity helps to explain the fact that there is little Georgian architecture in Ipswich.

In the early twentieth century, the largest wet dock in the Europe of the time was built there, and along with rail transport links for trade and the setting up of new industries during the Industrial Revolution, Ipswich was pulled into the modern world. This return to economic prosperity in turn produced much building in the Victorian period and many fine examples can still be seen in the town today.

The two World Wars of the twentieth century hit the town hard however. The excellent rail network, engineering works and the port were prime targets for German bombs. In the First World War several Zeppelin raids led to the destruction of many buildings, and in the Second World War the Luftwaffe carried out over fifty bombing raids over the town, which sadly resulted in dozens of deaths.

Football has long played a major part in town life, with Ipswich Town FC its focus, operating from the Portman Road stadium. The club can boast that it had the 1966 England World Cup winning manager Sir Alf Ramsey at the helm from 1955 until 1963. Ramsey took Ipswich Town to the top of the game, winning the First Division title in 1962. The pride and affection in which he is held are best symbolised by the elegant statue of him outside the ground. Ramsey continued to live in Ipswich until his death in April 1999.

All of these layers of history help to explain the sense of community to be found in Ipswich. The Suffolk character is simple and direct in the best possible sense. Honest, loyal and stubborn, the native Suffolk people embody the characteristics of an ancient community which has seen much change, but the direct approach to life has been passed down from generation to generation.

The people of Ipswich tend to take people at face value until given a reason not to, but there is an underlying core of shrewdness that should not be underestimated.

Through the addition to this native character of late twentieth- and early twenty-first-century immigration, a collective identity and a unique spirit have been forged. There is a definite provincial air in Ipswich, a feeling of self-reliance built through a tumultuous history. More intimate than a larger town or city, people communicate more and know more about each other. There is a feeling that there would be a 'pulling together' of the community in the face of collective adversity. This would be proven to be the case over those horrible weeks in December 2006, when at various moments time seemed to slow down, stand still and then race along.

For any loving parent, the death of a child is too frightening to imagine and even more painful in reality. When that child has predeceased a parent through a violent act, the hollow sense of loss is further complicated by powerful feelings of anger, frustration, bitterness and sometimes guilt. The cold reality of day is exposing and cruel. The parents of Gemma Adams now experienced this onslaught of emotions.

Like many parents they described their daughter as 'bright and bubbly' in media interviews. And photographs of Gemma certainly support this description. Blonde, blue-eyed and with a peachy complexion, her sweet smile makes her seem younger than her twenty-five years. She certainly does not look like the popular preconception of a prostitute, but then Gemma's background was very different from that of the 'average' prostitute.

In an interview with the *Daily Telegraph* on 12 December 2006, ten days after Gemma's body was pulled from Burstall Brook, her father Brian Adams expanded on his feelings for his daughter: 'We never knew she was working as a prostitute until she went missing. It's just every parent's worst nightmare. If we'd known, we would have done everything in our power to stop her, just like we tried to get her off drugs. But I don't want people to think of her only as a prostitute. The Gemma we want to remember was a loving, beautiful and wonderful girl.'

These are the moving words of a loving, heartbroken father, but of course the word that stands out is 'drugs'. And an examination of Gemma's upbringing makes her descent into addiction and then prostitution even more tragic. There were no underlying factors that could have predicted the route of her life. It must be remembered too that if she had had the chance to live, she may well have taken a better path in the future.

The Adams' family home is a large detached house in the wealthy village of Kesgrave, on the eastern fringes of Ipswich. Brian and Gail Adams have two other children apart from Gemma and they have all been brought up in a comfortable and loving environment. Gemma was always an animal-lover, very close to the family's pet dog Holly, and a keen horse rider. Like many young girls, Gemma was also a Brownie and thrived on group activities. As well as this she took piano lessons. It would be almost impossible to paint a rosier family portrait. There were never any signs in her childhood of what the future held for Gemma and she seemed destined for a bright future.

At the age of sixteen, Gemma left Kesgrave High

School, where she had been a popular student, and entered Suffolk College in Ipswich, a major educational and vocational training institution. Gemma completed a GNVQ course in Health and Social Care there.

But small cracks were beginning to appear in her life and her parents are sure that it was at about this time that she fell in with 'the wrong crowd'. In the *Sun* newspaper on 13 December, her father Brian said: 'She had everything going for her, yet at some point she was offered drugs, and it went from there.'

It seems that Gemma graduated from cannabis to heroin, and became quickly addicted. While the tabloid media tends to emphasise the link between these two drugs and liberal opinion likes to dissociate the two, in Gemma's case there was a definite escalation.

After leaving college, Gemma got a job at a local insurance company. But it was at this time in her early twenties that her heroin and crack cocaine addiction was beginning to take a firm hold. Her dependency soon became public knowledge at the insurance company as her attendance record rapidly worsened and when she was in the office she was sometimes not in a suitable state to fulfil her duties. She was eventually fired from the company in 2004.

This probably cut her final tie to the conventional life that she had aspired to as a girl and had been brought up to aim for. An addict needs their next fix and desperation usually leads to two well-trodden routes: burglary and prostitution. It seems that Gemma now took the latter option. By now Gemma was living away from her parents in rented accommodation in Ipswich with her boyfriend.

Her parents made numerous attempts to get her off

drugs, but they could not get through to her. Eventually they lost all contact with her. Their frustrated and loving need to help her was now permanently thwarted.

In the same interview, Brian Adams, fifty-three, said: 'Once your child is involved in hard drugs, your heart is already broken. It's just like we've been in a nightmare and even closing your eyes does not give you relief. You close your eyes and it's still there. Normally, if you have a nightmare, you wake up and the pain is gone, but this nightmare is ongoing.'

A moving tribute to Gemma was left on a local Ipswich newspaper's website during those terrible days. The poster was Gemma's sixteen-year-old brother Jack: 'Gem, you will never be forgotten. I know you're in a better place now, and I'll always love you. There is now a massive hole in our family that will never be filled.'

Touching words from a close-knit family now estranged from their beautiful sister and daughter forever. Her father Brian summed it all up in the *Sun* on 13 December: 'We are going through Hell. We are just praying that the madman who did this is caught soon.'

On the night of Tuesday, 14 November, Gemma and her boyfriend had left their home in Blenheim Road on the edge of Ipswich's red light district. They walked into one of the areas of the district where Gemma did business. She was soon alone on the streets. After the discovery of her body on 2 December, a witness came forward with the last known sighting of Gemma. This was at 1.15am on Wednesday 15 November outside a BMW car dealership on West End Road, close to the junction with Handford Road. The latter is a major road close to the Portman Road football stadium.

Gemma was reported missing at 2.55am, an hour and forty minutes after the last sighting. Her boyfriend Jon Simpson called the police after she had failed to respond to two text messages he had sent to her mobile phone. It would be seventeen days before her body was found 7 miles (11.3km) away.

The streets where Gemma spent her last free moments are tough ones. They are almost a universe away from the affluent village of Kesgrave where she was brought up. This network of streets near to the football ground would come under increasingly intense scrutiny over the following weeks. The spotlight would be firmly on this home of Ipswich subculture.

The red light district of Ipswich is situated to the west of the town centre itself, around the Portman Road football ground. The street that leads into the area from the main shopping centre has a seedy, neglected atmosphere. There are takeaway restaurants, tattoo and piercing parlours and small grocery shops. But the actual red light activities take place slightly further to the west, in what is primarily a residential area.

The houses here are in a variety of architectural styles, ranging greatly in size, age and price. A small network of streets and roads that are connected to and run between London Road, Handford Road and West End Road make up the red light area. London Road and Handford Road are also part of the A1214, which leads out of Ipswich and has good links to the A14 and A12. In this sense it is a crossroads area in and out of the town.

In the nineteenth century, when Ipswich was a busy port, there were almost forty brothels in the area, but there is nothing like that now. The overwhelming activity now is that of street prostitution and this is, as always, linked with drug dealing. A local resident of the Ipswich red light district says: 'I live in the red light area of Ipswich and regularly overhear early morning exchanges between local prostitutes, their dealers and the odd client.'

Of course, most of the kerb-crawling takes place in the twilight and dark and on most nights the classic image of a prostitute leaning into a car window can readily be seen. There are between thirty and forty prostitutes who regularly work in this area, despite police operations having cleared some streets.

Societies throughout history have never found a long-term solution for what is often called 'the oldest profession'. The dangers faced by these vulnerable women (and sometimes men) are massive. There are the obvious dangers of physical attack and sexually transmitted diseases, but also the hidden risks of psychological damage. The trigger for entry into 'the game' is usually desperation for money. But there are other factors that keep prostitutes working: a single parent needing to support children, fear of violence from a pimp or trafficking gang, and drugs. It is the last of these that saturates this story.

Drug addiction, specifically of the Class A kind, is a terrible sickness. The habit must be fed, the next fix paid for by any means necessary. Sometimes a habit can be exorbitantly expensive, and the relatively high and immediate payment that prostitution offers is often the only way an addict feels they can survive. Drug dealers are only too aware of this and so where there are prostitutes there are usually drug dealers, and vice versa. This is the case in the red light district of Ipswich.

If drugs are the root cause of much prostitution, then that is the problem that our society has to tackle. Especially in a rich country such as Britain – collectively as a nation we have let these human beings down. Vulnerable and fragile people cannot survive intact in a harsh, predatory environment; a snowball does not stand a chance in an oven.

According to Home Office figures, sixty prostitutes are known to have been murdered in Britain in the decade between 1996 and 2006 – an average of six a year, or one every two months. In 2006 alone, there were 766 known murders in Britain and 2.4 million violent attacks. The UK achieved an impressive murder conviction rate in 2006 of over 75 per cent. But the UK murder conviction rate where the victims were prostitutes was only 26 per cent for the same year.

On the very day that Gemma Adams took her last walk to work in Ipswich's red light district, Tuesday 14 November 2006, there was a news item on page fifteen of the Ipswich *Evening Star*, the headline reading 'Campaign on Prostitution a Failure – Claim'. Gemma would be reported missing within hours of this edition of the newspaper going on sale.

As recorded on the Ipswich Labour Party's website, a survey had been carried out in August 2006 by Labour Party councillors and Chris Mole, MP. The results showed that '90% of people living in and around Ipswich's red light district said their lives were affected by street prostitution'. Prompted by this finding the Labour Group called on Ipswich Borough Council, Suffolk County Council, the primary care trust and Suffolk Police to crack down on street prostitution.

Three months later, the leader of the Labour Group, Councillor David Ellesmere, reported that 'the response had been disappointing'.

Councillor Ellesmere said: 'Leading politicians at the borough and county councils do not appear to have taken much interest in the issue. There has been little or no action on the majority of our proposed programme. No mobile CCTV cameras have been deployed, there's been no commitment to a programme of alley-gating, no improvement on reporting procedures for prostitution and kerb-crawling, no increase in cleaning resources or improvement in reporting procedures for needles and condoms, no increase in the use of ASBOs (Anti-Social Behaviour Orders) for offenders and no extra help to get women out of prostitution or increased drug treatment.'

Councillor Ellesmere did however reserve some praise for Suffolk Police, saying that visible patrols had increased and some plain-clothes work had started. This was the state of affairs when Gemma Adams disappeared.

In the *Guardian* newspaper of 22 March 2007, Liz Harsant, the leader of Ipswich Borough Council, was reported as saying: 'The red light district is actually a nice residential area and many of the residents have had enough of the girls, the needles, the foul language and fights.' She went on to say that Ipswich Borough Council was now taking 'a zero tolerance approach' to street prostitution. By July 2007 more CCTV and better lighting had been installed in the red light district.

But by then it was eight months too late.

The discovery of the body of Gemma Adams made the front page of the Ipswich *Evening Star*, under the headline

'Somebody's Daughter'. A shockwave went around the local community, especially in Hintlesham where she was found.

But at this stage it seemed like an isolated event. A woman had been murdered, a prostitute. There probably would have been greater fear if the woman had not been a prostitute. Some people see working girls as putting themselves in the path of danger on a daily basis. The same had been seen in the hunt for the Yorkshire Ripper, Peter Sutcliffe, more than twenty-five years earlier. Sutcliffe had brutally murdered thirteen women and attacked seven others, most of them prostitutes. There had been real terror on city streets in Yorkshire at the time. But this fear had escalated as soon as he killed his first non-prostitute victim.

However, the people of Ipswich were taken aback by the sheer callous inhumanity of how Gemma was found, discarded like a shop dummy from last season. It was a talking point in local shops, offices and at bus stops. The anguish of the Adams family touched many hearts. There was also some moralising and smug self-assurance. Other prostitutes were realising that it was probably bad luck that had singled out Gemma. It could have been them.

As well as establishing 'no definitive cause of death', the post-mortem examination on Gemma was able to conclude that there had been no sexual assault. The fact that the body had been found naked pointed to a sexual murder, but Suffolk Police were now having to consider different options. There were also many questions to be answered. Did the killer have consensual sex with Gemma as a business transaction before killing her? What was the motive? Was she left in the brook immediately after death? Was there a connection to a regular punter?

Detective Chief Inspector David Skevington of Suffolk Police made the routine appeal for information in a murder inquiry. He said: 'Further enquiries need to be carried out to ascertain how long Gemma had been in the water, but our appeals are to anyone who had been in the area of Thorpes Hill in Hintlesham in the past two-and-a-half weeks since Gemma went missing on November 14.'

It was also stated that as she had been found unclothed it was a 'matter of urgency' that they find her clothing. The clothes worn by Gemma on the night of her disappearance were as follows: a black waterproof waist-length jacket with a hood and a zip at the front, light blue jeans with studs on the pockets, a red top and white and chrome Nike trainers. Gemma had been carrying a black handbag, but this had been found close to the crime scene. The contents of the handbag were a toothbrush, a tube of toothpaste and a change of knickers.

Posters went up with Gemma's photograph and description. On 5 December the police made a further appeal for information from the public and urged Gemma's clients to make contact with them. Regular clients needed to be eliminated from the inquiry, but of course this was a very sensitive matter for the men concerned. Other prostitutes from the red light district were also questioned, many of whom knew Gemma. The police knew that the smallest, most trivial piece of information might lead to the killer.

Searches were also made of the red light district itself, within a specified radius from where Gemma was last seen. Door-to-door enquiries of the local area were carried out in case any local residents had seen or heard something and not yet come forward. The white and chrome Nike trainers that Gemma had been wearing were found near a tyre-fitting firm about a mile (1.6km) from the red light district. But there was no sign of her other clothes.

There was no breakthrough clue, no piece of information giving the police a name or an address. But there were leads and these had to be followed up.

On Saturday 5 December the national press began to take notice. The reason was a chilling one – there were concerns for another young Ipswich woman working as a prostitute. There was a very small report in the *Sun* newspaper about police fears for missing Tania Nicol, aged nineteen.

Tania had worked the same streets of the Ipswich red light district as Gemma. Police were quoted as saying that there were 'obvious similarities' between Gemma's murder and Tania's disappearance. Tania Nicol had gone missing on Monday 30 October. That was five weeks ago and more than two weeks before Gemma had disappeared. Where could she be?

Tania had last been seen on that Monday night at 11.02pm. She had been recorded on CCTV outside Sainsburys supermarket in London Road, Ipswich at that time. This is in the red light district. Before that, she had last been seen leaving home at 10.30pm to work the streets. Tania had been reported missing by her mother on Wednesday 1 November.

Police, family and friends had been trying to find her since then, but the discovery of Gemma's body had made tracing her far more urgent. The fact that both Gemma and Tania were working as prostitutes in the same area, perhaps sometimes sharing the same clients, did not make the police feel optimistic. Five weeks is a long time to be missing when there is no apparent reason.

It soon became clear that Gemma and Tania had been friends. This was not so surprising, as they must have seen each other regularly. Detective Superintendent Andrew Henwood of Suffolk Police said: 'We are still treating Tania's disappearance as a separate inquiry, but we have grave concerns for her.'

Sadly those concerns would soon prove to be well placed.

CHAPTER TWO

THE TRAGEDY
DEEPENS

The appeals to locate Tania Nicol were now stepped up by the Suffolk Police. Posters and leaflets showing Tania's photograph were distributed. Having left her home in Woolverstone Close in the Pinebrook area of Ipswich, south-west of the town centre on 30 October 2006, it was learnt that Tania had planned to take a bus from nearby Belmont Road into Ipswich. She intended to work the streets that night.

The CCTV footage from all relevant buses was checked, but the police were unable to trace her movements. It could not be proved whether Tania ever did get on to a bus.

In the first week of November 2006, almost a month before the body of Gemma Adams was found, Detective Chief Inspector John Quinton had said: 'There have been some unconfirmed sightings in the Ipswich area around the time Tania went missing last week. Also, a number of her associates have come forward. This has all provided information for the inquiry team to follow up.'

However, there were no strong leads to her whereabouts until after Gemma Adams was found in Belstead Brook. The police then changed the direction of the Tania Nicol inquiry, which was still officially a missing person investigation. The links between Gemma and Tania now heightened police fears and a new focus was employed in the hunt for Tania.

By trawling through hours and hours of CCTV footage from Ipswich's red light district, the police were able to identify Tania Nicol on captures taken at 11.02pm on 30 October, walking past the exit of the Sainsburys garage on London Road, and then around five minutes later at the junction of nearby Handford Road and Burlington Road.

The police description issued by Suffolk Police was as follows: 'Tania is described as olive-skinned, 5ft 2in tall (1.57m), slim build, with shoulder-length, light brown hair, brown eyes and a spotty complexion. The clothes which Tania wore on the last night she was seen were a black jacket, mid-blue cut-off jeans, a light-coloured top and pink sparkly high-heeled shoes.'

On Thursday, 7 December, the police released a photograph of a pair of shoes similar to the ones she was wearing. As DCI John Quinton said: 'As part of our enquiries we have been working with a company to get a photo of the same shoes Tania was known to be wearing the night she went missing. We know New Look manufactured the shoes and they are very distinctive, having a pink sparkly appearance, a small buckle and high stiletto heels. It is imperative that we try to work out Tania's movements on the night she went missing – we hope that by issuing the picture of the shoes, someone's memory will be jogged and they will remember seeing her that evening or since.'

The last word of this statement shows that the police did believe that she could still be alive. But it was now five weeks since she was last seen and five days since the body of Gemma Adams had been discovered. No confirmed sightings, no word from Tania herself (this was out of character for her), and the murder of a woman who had known Tania and had plied the same trade in the same area. And Gemma had been missing for a shorter length of time than Tania. It was little wonder that optimism was dwindling.

This was driven home further when the police began searching intensely in the back streets and alleyways of the red light district where Tania was last recorded being, as well as in gardens and outbuildings of both residential and business sites across Ipswich. It would not be long before a development occurred, but tragically it was to be the worst one possible.

The long weeks since Tania had gone missing were of course extremely emotionally draining for her loved ones. At times of great apprehension such as that, it is hard enough getting through the day, let alone the night. At such times the true value of family and friends is shown, as a strong, mutually supportive phalanx is formed.

For Tania's father, Jim Duell, religion was a huge comfort. A born-again Christian, Mr Duell found solace in faith. In an interview with BBC Suffolk, he said: 'When she went missing I had to go down to Wiltshire. As I drove down there they had the posters going up – that she'd gone missing – and that really sunk in what had happened. The reality of it hit me.'

Mr Duell then went on to describe a religious vision he had had regarding his daughter: 'That night, about five in the morning, I got up and I actually was praying. What I got from that was God saying to me, "I'm going to give you a foundation to walk on"'.

Mr Duell would go on to have a vision which gave him hope that Tania was at peace, despite hinting that she was dead: 'I had a vision of a really thick piece of rope being broken, and I could see the frayed ends of this rope. All I could see behind that was gold. And I had the same vision the next night.'

Jim Duell interpreted this vision as 'Tania's lifeline being snapped', which of course meant the end of her life. When he went to church the following Sunday he told everyone about the vision he had had and the meaning he took from it, but then he had a further personal revelation: 'When I sat down, I thought "Just a minute, it means something else". It means that all the sin, all the horribleness [sic] that she got herself involved in, the Lord removed all that away from her and took her into his heart. That was a huge relief to me. I was worried about her soul.'

This vision gave Mr Duell great strength in the upcoming weeks, strength that would be greatly needed.

FRIDAY, 8 DECEMBER 2006
COPDOCK MILL, SUFFOLK
11.30am
The village of Copdock Mill is just south of Hintlesham, where Gemma Adams was found. The two villages are connected by Belstead Brook, and this waterway runs all

the way east to the River Orwell, around 7 (11.3km) away to the south of Ipswich itself. The police were using divers to search Belstead Brook in the hope of finding some of Gemma's clothing. They were also still looking for Tania Nicol at this time, but did not expect to find her there.

Yet at 11.30am on 8 December they did just that. Close to the business premises of HG Gladwell & Sons, about 1.5 miles (2.4km) downstream from where Gemma had been discovered six days earlier, they found the naked body of Tania Nicol. She was lying in what amounted to little more than a pond. She was formally identified the following day.

The way in which both Gemma and Tania had been left, both naked, and in such close proximity to each other, pointed to the possibility of a serial offender or offenders at work and though the police kept this to themselves, immediate appeals were made for information. Detective Chief Inspector John Quinton said that the two bodies may have been dumped together, but then added: 'The brook is fast flowing and the most recent body could have been carried from elsewhere.'

Detective Superintendent Andy Henwood said: 'Enquiries are continuing to try to ascertain where and when Tania's and Gemma's bodies were placed in the water and the circumstances of their deaths.'

Again the area was thoroughly searched and the forensic team went to work. The scenes-of-crime officers looked for any microscopic samples of blood, semen, hair and fibres left by the killer. Any such evidence could help to build a DNA profile. In addition, any shoe or tyre prints as well as fingerprints could have been crucial evidence.

The post-mortem on Tania again failed to pinpoint a definite cause of death, and there were no obvious injuries to her body. Nevertheless the forensic team hoped that the toxicology reports would provide some answers.

One factor that the police were very aware of was that the bodies being found in water would affect their chances of getting a solid DNA profile. The water could have destroyed any crucial evidence. The killer might have chosen Belstead Brook as a dumping ground for this very reason. Or perhaps it was just luck. Also, the length of time between the disappearances of the girls and the discovery of their bodies (six weeks in Tania's case) meant that essential evidence could have been lost or contaminated.

With another stretch of earthy Suffolk countryside sealed off, the local and national reaction began to build. As Sarah Barber, a Copdock sub-postmistress, said: 'It's shocking. A lot of children play in the area.'

Though not as shocking as it was for those who knew and loved Tania Nicol.

Tania Nicol came from a far less financially privileged background than Gemma Adams. She grew up on a housing estate on the outskirts of Ipswich, and despite her parents splitting up, she was well loved and had a stable home life. On the night that she disappeared, Monday 30 October, she had left the home on the housing estate she shared with her mother Kerry and fifteen-year-old brother Aaron. Friends were to describe the family as inseparable.

At the age of nineteen, Tania was still little more than a girl when she died. Memories of her held by the people who knew and loved her are touching and reveal a young woman who was excited by music, fashion and hairdressing, a girl with normal interests whose young energy and sense of fun made an impression on all those around her.

Her mother Kerry told the *Sun* newspaper: 'We were always together when Tania was growing up. She was a real "girlie" girl, not a tomboy at all. She loved playing in the sand, and we'd take trips to the beach at Felixstowe.'

Almost ten years of age when the all-female pop group the Spice Girls were launched on to the cultural scene in 1996, the young Tania idolised the five singers and dancers who represented 'girl power'. Like millions of other little girls, Tania was inspired and electrified by their potent energy. One can imagine her singing into her hairbrush in front of the mirror, impersonating her role models, giving her the confidence to express her own identity, which of course was still forming.

While attending Chantry High School in Ipswich, Tania had heartfelt dreams of becoming a pop star like her idols. Her friend since childhood, Susie Coburn, remembered her: 'A bunch of us used to hang out together, going to each other's houses and staying over. Tania loved music and when the Spice Girls came out she just loved everything they did. She was obsessed by them and wore Spice Girls earrings. She was always very funny.'

Like many girls, Tania loved to dress up, have her face painted and try out new hairstyles. She began to show a real interest in becoming a hairdresser, a job that needs impeccable social skills as well as technical ability, and Tania definitely possessed the former. She was constantly trying out new hairstyles on her friends. She was a popular student at school, with a very caring personality evidenced by her love of cats.

Tania's bright and sunny personality seemed set to serve her well in facing life's ups and downs and her economically tough start had made her a resilient yet sensitive young woman. However, teenage years are times of great change for any child as the adult personality begins to emerge, and in her late teens Tania began to be rebellious.

It started by Tania's staying out late and sometimes lying to her mother about where she was going and where she had been. After school, a series of poorly paid jobs followed, including one at an Ipswich hotel. The dreams of pop stardom were giving way to the realities of life.

It cannot be said for certain at what age Tania drifted into drug use and prostitution, but it was certainly around this time. It is known that she worked at several massage parlours in Ipswich. The owner of one of the parlours, a woman called Sandra, told the Ipswich *Evening Star* that Tania had worked for her. Sandra said that Tania's mother Kerry had previously worked there as a cleaner, but not at the same time that her daughter was offering other services there. Sandra said that in the end she had to ask Tania to leave as she suspected that she was using drugs: 'She was a placid and quiet girl and took the news that she had to leave very well.'

Holly, a former schoolfriend of Tania, who was working at another massage parlour when she spoke to the same newspaper, was very surprised to find out in April 2006 that Tania was working on the streets. This is of course far more dangerous and less hygienic than working in a parlour. But then perhaps Tania had had little choice because of her drug use. Holly said: 'It seemed totally out of character for her, she was a truly wonderful girl, so quiet and nice to everyone. She was so pretty and always wore nice clothes.'

It is true that Tania had an almost classical beauty; the long, angular face and dark features with dark eyes and striking black hair are very distinctive in her photographs. The writer Libby Purves has described Tania as looking like a 'Renaissance angel'. This seems a fitting description.

Although the link between hard drug use and prostitution can be made here, at the time of her disappearance, unlike Gemma Adams, Tania was still living at home. However, her mother and brother had no idea about her activities as a prostitute, and it seems that Tania kept the two parts of her life very separate. Her mother Kerry told the *Sun*: 'She got in with the wrong crowd and that should be a warning to anyone. I knew nothing of her secret life until the police told me. I'm finding it hard to come to terms with her getting into cars with strangers. To me and Aaron she was a caring member of our family. Seeing her being labelled a prostitute is horrible and makes her seem like she's not a person.'

The media loves labels, and most coverage would emphasise the prostitution angle. But to get a true sense of Tania, the online condolence book set up on the website of the Ipswich *Evening Star* is helpful. Family, friends and acquaintances left messages of affection and loss:

'I am Tania's grandmother. Me and my other children are very upset by the news of her death. She was a very beautiful woman and had everything to live for.'
'Tania was my beautiful niece. She was loved by all our family. I just can't understand why some evil

27

person would want to hurt her and her friend. I hope the police catch whoever did this soon.'

'I knew Tania when we were younger, and we had some good times. I remember making up dances with her... She was a beautiful young girl, very smiley, and wouldn't hurt anyone.'

'Tania used to braid my hair when I was pregnant. She was so talented. A group of us went on holiday to the New Forest and had such a laugh. She was such an outgoing, loving girl.'

'I would just like to say how sad it is to hear about Tania. She often walked past my house and she went through school with my daughter of the same age. I did not know her personally but she will be missed. My thoughts are with her family.'

For Tania's father, Jim Duell, comfort could only come from a higher source. The pure evil that had befallen his daughter could only be rationalised by his Christian beliefs. The religious vision he had had made him sure that God had been with Tania at the end. Mr Duell told BBC Suffolk: 'In that moment of fear and terror that Tania must have been going through, He intervened.'

Mr Duell turned to the Bible to help console himself and Tania's friends in church as they prayed for Tania after her body was discovered. He said: 'I read in John 14 that when Jesus was explaining to his disciples that something was going to happen to Jesus, that he was about to leave them, they couldn't comprehend that. What he said was, "When I go you will have a helper, the counsellor will come to you. I have to do this in order for you to have this helper – which is the Holy Spirit".'

Jim Duell related this to Tania's friends to offer them comfort in their grief and shock. He explained: 'I wanted to get the message across to all her friends at church that the holy spirit does all the workings on this earth and that Tania was rescued from her own self, and that she's safe and well.'

In the weeks and months after his daughter's murder, Mr Duell was able to find solace and emotional support in his faith. He continued: 'When I became a born-again Christian I was given a peace. I experienced a peace that you can't get at Tesco, you can't get it at the Post Office, you can't get it at the bank. You can't fill in an application form for it. It's a peace given by God – as Jesus says "I give to you a peace that the world cannot give".'

Murder is one of the hardest events that loved ones and friends could ever have to deal with. Whether interpreted as an act of compassionate rescue by God or an act of cold-blooded evil by a killer perhaps does not really matter. The fact is that the murder occurred and the powerful emotions of loss, anger and bitterness have to be dealt with. Getting through it is surely all that is important in the end.

It was becoming clear by this stage that there was a serial element to the murders. Both Gemma Adams and Tania Nicol had been found naked, in the same waterway and geographically close together and neither had any visible external injuries. This is one of the stranger aspects of the killings – they were not bloody or gruesome, but clinical and callous. There was a dark psychopathic edge to them: a total lack of conventional conscience or empathy for other human beings; a cold-blooded detachment. The way in which the victims were dumped, naked to the elements, but lying apparently peacefully, almost as if sleeping, is perhaps just as unsettling as an emotional, frenzied attack.

The fact that Gemma and Tania worked as street prostitutes in the same red light area of Ipswich, knew each other, and perhaps sometimes had the same clients is also revealing. For a murderer with a sexual motive, prostitutes are naturally easy targets. With their professional activities technically illegal in Britain, it is often necessary for street prostitutes to carry out their transactions in secluded, lonely places. Inevitably this compromises them and if a client's motives are violent or murderous there is little chance of escape or rescue.

Every serial killer has a modus operandi, a way of working, and this particular killer's method appeared to be highly efficient. When profiling, some experts divide killers into two broad groups based on the killer's methods and the meticulous analysis of any unusual quirks they may display. Through the way they operate, a killer can reveal a great deal about their personality, needs and motives.

The two general groups into which a killer can be placed first are 'organised' or 'disorganised'. The organised killer will probably have reasonably logical thought processes and show a degree of planning, premeditation or forethought. The disorganised killer is more irregular in his thought processes, is more impulsive and may display more obvious signs of mental illness. He is usually more random in his targets, or perhaps kills in a frenzy, with emotion much more evident in his profile. Sometimes, a killer can fit both of these profiles. The

Whitechapel murderer of 1888, 'Jack the Ripper', is one such example. Although his murders (of at least five London prostitutes) were carried out in a frenzied way, with much mutilation, there was a method to his particular madness. He removed internal organs from several victims, and did it so expertly that he was thought to have medical knowledge.

The way in which Jack the Ripper chose his targets and knew his murderous patch was also highly organised. He managed to evade capture every time, despite there being a huge police presence on the streets as the terror grew. A disorganised killer would probably have been caught. But the last murder committed by Jack the Ripper, that of Mary Kelly in Miller's Court, appeared to be very disorganised. The level of frenzy was almost unbelievable and contemporary police photographs of the crime scene reveal a scene of unimaginable horror. This was the only murder he committed indoors, so he had more time to carry out his terrible mutilations, but the escalation of violence suggests that his mind may have given way. This could explain why this was the last murder, if afterwards the killer had either been committed to a mental asylum or had committed suicide.

The modus operandi of the Ipswich killer was of course very different. All of the traits and methods this killer displayed pointed to an organised offender, especially in the disposal of the bodies. Whether he knew the women as a client or stalked and selected them over a period of time was not known. However, a key issue was the long length of time that elapsed between the disappearances of Gemma and Tania and the discovery of their bodies, just over two weeks and five weeks respectively, and this had to be explained. Where had they been in the interim?

It was not known exactly how long the bodies had been in Belstead Brook, but neither of the bodies showed an advanced state of decomposition. Had they been kept alive in captivity before being killed, or murdered immediately and then stored (perhaps in a freezer to preserve the bodies) and dumped later? This could not be ascertained at this stage, but another serial murder case from the past can perhaps offer some insight and throw up some parallels.

The series of murders in question are known as the 'Jack the Stripper' murders or the 'Thames Nude' murders. They took place between 1959 and 1964, a five-year period. Although this is a far longer time span than that of the Ipswich murders, there are some similarities.

There were eight murders committed by Jack the Stripper in West London and some victims were found in the River Thames. All of the women had been prostitutes and all were found completely naked or almost naked, just as in Ipswich. The key features of the case were that many victims had had some teeth removed by the killer and specks of spray paint were found on some bodies.

It was obvious to the police at the time that the women had not been killed where they were found, but had died somewhere else and then been dumped. But there had to have been a storage place. The spots of paint on some bodies pointed to a paint spray workshop.

Although forensic science was far less advanced at that time than in 2006, it was soon worked out how they had died. The women had died from asphyxiation and this helped to explain the killer's modus operandi. The prostitutes were almost all picked up in the area of West London between Notting Hill and Hammersmith, and then taken somewhere in a vehicle, probably a van (a white van had been spotted several times by witnesses). The women were probably then asked to perform oral sex on their client. While she was in the necessary crouching position, the killer forced the woman's head down on to his penis, and she choked, leading to asphyxiation. After that, the victim would then have been taken to a hiding place, probably in or close to a paint spray workshop. There he would force out some of the victim's teeth and carry out acts of oral rape post-mortem. After his depraved fantasies were satisfied, the body was driven away and dumped.

This is a scenario that could possibly be similar to that of the Ipswich murders. The lack of injuries on both Gemma and Tania pointed to an organised killer who must have had somewhere to take the victims. There are many differences between the two cases – not least the length of time over which the murders were carried out. Those committed by Jack the Stripper spanned years, whereas the Ipswich killings merely weeks. But the parallels are there. In both cases, the victims were prostitutes working the streets. The victims were found naked and with no visible wounds (apart from the teeth extraction in the earlier case). There was undoubtedly a storage place for the bodies before being dumped (and perhaps where other fantasies were carried out) and both cases showed a killer who liked to leave the bodies of his victims in or close to water.

But above all, the earlier case is useful in showing us the temperament of such a killer. Highly organised and efficient, even the teeth extraction carried out by Jack the Stripper can be seen as practical for his terrible purposes. Likewise the Ipswich offender or offenders showed a remarkable coolness and confidence in his modus operandi. It was almost as if the killer was showing how clever he was.

Nobody was ever convicted for the Jack the Stripper murders but the police were sure they knew who the killer was. Their investigation had managed to focus on three main suspects. Then one of the three committed suicide. He was an unmarried security guard who worked at night and whose patrol included a paint spray workshop. The suicide note that he left said that he could not take the strain any more. There were no more murders after that.

But the police investigating the Ipswich murders had none of the benefits of hindsight. They were now almost certain that they were tracking a serial killer or killers who could strike again at any time. This put the inquiry under tremendous time pressure.

The nature of a serial killer inquiry before the offender is caught is a fraught business. The police are thrown into unknown territory, as although much has been learnt from other investigations in Britain and at the FBI base at Quantico, with effective procedures adopted as a result, there is nonetheless no one blueprint for such a killer or killers. Each serial inquiry must be approached on an individual basis. Although the acts committed by the perpetrator may seem inhuman, they were carried out by a human being and people come in all shapes and sizes, just as human nature works in numerous shades of grey.

The logistics of such an investigation are enormously

complex in terms of manpower, resources and approach. It is crucial to have a firm hand and a well-defined investigative direction, yet with a degree of flexibility and pragmatism, backed up by the effective use of limited manpower and delegation. Working against a racing clock and with no knowledge of whether tomorrow will unearth another victim, the pressure is unrelenting – and amplified in the 24/7 media age of the twenty-first century.

The Suffolk Constabulary is one of the smallest police forces in Britain, and with the discovery of two victims in six days, the scale of what it would take to apprehend the killer or killers was just dawning. With a working police force of just 1,300 officers, the resources of the Suffolk Police would be greatly stretched. Fortunately help would be forthcoming from other constabularies and Scotland Yard itself.

But it is the unknown that is the most difficult factor for any police force to deal with. In an interview with the author, a local man who has lived in Ipswich all of his life said: 'It's off everybody's radar – you can't forecast an event like this. You can only prepare for what you know is a day-to-day happening, like, you know, when the football happens, and have extra guys on hand. You can't legislate for an unknown maniac on the loose. He could strike in any town, or any county.'

Recent serial investigations gave the police skills and pointers in how to approach such an inquiry. The Soham murders of 2002, which took place just over the border in Cambridgeshire, are just such an example. The tragic murders of the little girls Holly Wells and Jessica Chapman prompted a similarly intensive manhunt before the school caretaker Ian Huntley was arrested, charged and convicted. Likewise, the investigations of the serial murders of Fred and Rosemary West, arrested in the 1990s, provided some procedural approaches.

Technology has advanced such large-scale inquiries a great deal. It has managed to help the police avoid the logistical and administrative errors which, among other factors, allowed the Yorkshire Ripper Peter Sutcliffe to slip through detection nets and continue killing, before he was finally caught in a fateful moment of luck for the police. The use of computers instead of thousands of paper filing cards has solved many such cross-referencing problems. Sutcliffe had been interviewed at least twice during the inquiry, and a computerised system would most probably have exposed the links he had with the inquiry and led to his arrest much more quickly.

Learning from mistakes on previous inquiries and adapting available technology to the needs of the cases were crucial now for the Suffolk Police. All police forces in Britain now use the *Murder Investigation Manual*, and the first step this illustrates is how to assemble an expert team of analysts. The prioritisation and clarification of information are their task. This information is then entered into a unique and independent database, the Home Office Large Major Enquiry System (HOLMES). This system is a masterpiece of criminal cross-referencing and will expose any relevant links. The use of a computer timeline by the inquiry team allows it to see all the most important pieces of gathered information, and when used with i2 software, trends and themes can be spotted.

In any modern investigation, the work of forensic teams is of course vital. The use of DNA profiles and any other evidence left by the killer is of paramount importance. However, the long delay in the discovery of the bodies of Gemma Adams and Tania Nicol, added to the fact that their bodies were left in water, meant that there was little forensic evidence. Water destroys some forensic traces, and the killer may or may not have known this.

Much is said about the negative implications of our 'surveillance society', with its echoes of Orwell's 'Big Brother'. Yet it is a fact that CCTV footage and the ability to attain zoomed frames to capture detail are very helpful to any police investigation. Officers were already poring over hours and hours of footage taken in the Ipswich red light district and the surrounding area, and also that from cameras placed on the A14 and A12 roads, the main roads leading to the sites where the women were found.

The use of national databases also enabled the police to locate almost 400 registered sex offenders living in Suffolk. The Soham murders had led to a much more formal way of registering such offenders and this was an obvious starting point for the Suffolk Police. Neither Gemma nor Tania was sexually assaulted and this did confuse the inquiry a little. Nevertheless the fact that they were found naked did point to a sexual motive of some sort. Any other linked attacks documented by other police forces also had to be looked into, in case of any connections with the current cases.

The fact that the murders of Tania and Gemma had occurred so quickly in succession (it appeared that Tania was probably killed first, but found second) was also unusual. Most serial killers leave a long space of time between their first and second murders. This is often largely due to them coming to terms with what they have done and trying to control themselves to stop it happening again. The ones who cannot suppress the murderous urge become serial offenders. But the gap between the virgin kill and the second murder is often many months or years. With the Ipswich murders, it was weeks, with a definite 'spree' element, which only heightened police concerns.

This consequently led to informed speculation that these were not the first and second murders committed by the killer. Therefore, earlier unsolved cases were looked into, especially those within a geographical radius or catchment area of Ipswich. Several such unsolved cases were reinvestigated, stretching back as far as 1992.

In 2002, the body of twenty-two-year-old Michelle Bettles was found in Dereham after she vanished from Norwich's red light district. She had been strangled. In 2000, Kellie Pratt, twenty-nine, disappeared from the same area. She was never found. A year earlier in 1999, seventeen-year-old Vicky Hall, a student, vanished on her way home in Trimley St Mary near Ipswich. Her body was discovered in Stowmarket in Suffolk. A man accused of her murder was acquitted in 2001. In 1993, the body of Mandy Duncan, twenty-six, from Woodbridge, Suffolk, was never found. She had disappeared from the Ipswich red light district. Finally, there was sixteen-year-old Natalie Pearman, whose body was found at a beauty spot outside Norwich in 1992. She had been strangled and had last been seen in the Norwich red light area.

The police stated that they had not managed to find any conclusive evidence to link these earlier crimes with the Ipswich murders yet. However, there are some obvious similarities. The city of Norwich is 43 miles (69km) north of Ipswich and the connection between the two places would later have some significance as the Ipswich nightmare progressed. Had the Ipswich killer struck before? If so, how many times, when and where?

Geographical clues can also provide many leads in profiling such a killer or killers. The world renowned criminal psychologist and profiler Professor David Canter says in his book *Mapping Murder*: 'Criminals reveal who they are and where they live not just from how they commit their crimes but also from the locations they choose.'

As both Gemma and Tania were left close to the A14 and A12 roads, this probably had some significance. For this reason, the police were also looking at possible suspects in the towns of Colchester and Felixstowe, which lie at opposite ends of the A14. On the other hand, it could just as well have been a person or persons local to Ipswich who knew the area very well. The bodies were only dumped in Belstead Brook: the actual murders and possibly storage took place somewhere else.

It has to be remembered that much of the police work in such a large investigation is still old-fashioned detective work, and often a sheer grind. In any murder inquiry, the police will primarily look at the victims and the people who surrounded them in life, from family and friends to slight acquaintances. It is a sad fact that the majority of murder victims are killed by people they know. In a serial case, the police have to establish any 'commonalities' between the victims also; in other words, all of the links between them. Any common ties between Gemma and Tania, whether it be friends, clients or a drug dealer, were an essential starting point.

The same amount of thorough detective work, appeals

and interviews had to be carried out with regard to witnesses. As shown, door-to-door interviews and requests for information, as well as television and other media appeals, are important in such a case. Fellow prostitutes and clients who came forward or were traced were all interviewed. The police needed as coherent and detailed a picture as possible of the two women: their lives, contacts and last movements. This was painstaking work but absolutely crucial, as a tiny fact can lead to an arrest.

In overall command of the Ipswich murders inquiry was the Chief Constable of Suffolk, Alistair McWhirter, now retired from the force. Deputy Chief Constable Jacqui Cheer dealt with operational aspects. But the officer in charge of the inquiry on the ground was Detective Chief Superintendent Stewart Gull, a very experienced police officer. He can have had little doubt about the nature of the daunting task he faced, especially as local fears and media interest increased. The spotlight was focusing on Ipswich.

The fact that Tania Nicol had been missing for five weeks had made little impact on the local community despite police appeals throughout November. But the discovery of the body of Gemma Adams on 2 December had increased local concerns about Tania, and the subsequent finding of her body on 8 December changed local perceptions a great deal. In the space of six days, two local women had been found dead, in similar circumstances and in close proximity to each other.

As the Christmas advent calendar windows began to be opened daily and the festive holiday dominated minds, this sudden and unusual darkness began to descend on Ipswich, and a town that was usually only mentioned on a national level in relation to the football scores was thrust into the limelight. No place wants to be famous for the murders that occur there. Infamy of that kind is never welcomed. In a large city, such a case would have made an impact, but perhaps the size of the place and the impersonal hustle and bustle of city life could have absorbed the shock better. There was to be no escape for the people of Ipswich – this fear would seep into the skin of every local person over the next two weeks.

The local media, both television and newspaper, had been following developments since Gemma was discovered on 2 December. But the national media had shown only passing interest until Tania was found on 8 December. Any scent of a serial killer on the loose had woken up the national press and television news networks. Since the highly publicised hunt for the Yorkshire ripper in the late 1970s and early 1980s, serial murder cases have been avidly followed by the British media. The element of suspense and the looming of a dark shadow over ordinary society obviously appeal to both viewers and readers.

The Hollywood film of the early 1990s, 'The Silence of the Lambs', about a fictional serial killer, helped to cement the concept of the serial murderer in the public consciousness, and since then many other films about real and imaginary serial killers have appeared. In terms of the British media, cases such as the Soham murders, the Fred and Rosemary West murders and the frighteningly prolific killing spree of 'Dr Death', Harold Shipman, all attracted huge media interest. And it was now becoming clear that the Ipswich murders would be no different.

The first sign came on the day after Tania's body was

found, when the *Sun*, Britain's biggest selling newspaper, put the story on the front page. The headline was 'New Vice Girl Victim of Ripper'. Continuing inside the paper the story was headed with 'Prostitutes in Ipswich Fear a Ripper-Style Killer is on the Prowl'. Included in this report on 9 December was an interview with an Ipswich prostitute who did not want to be named. She was quoted as saying: 'We're all afraid there's a maniac on the loose. People feared the worst when Gemma and Tania went missing. Now another body's been found, that fear has turned to panic.'

At this stage there were still prostitutes working on the streets of the Ipswich red light district, but the tension and fear were obviously growing amongst them. Two of their number going missing was one thing – and frightening enough. But the discovery of the bodies of the two women was something else and it confirmed that the killer was targeting prostitutes.

It could be said that the high profile beginning to be given to the murders by the media was feeding this fear, but on the other hand the public have a right to be kept informed if there is a dangerous killer or killers at large. The target group of prostitutes was of course under the biggest threat, but there was no reason to think that the killer would not choose a non-prostitute victim at some point, just as the Yorkshire Ripper Peter Sutcliffe had done. As a local resident told this author: 'The worry was that the guy doing this was going to move sideways, from prostitutes – not, I hasten to add that that makes any difference. But if he's moved away from that focused target to women in general, that was the worry.'

An interesting point is that the national tabloid media

liked to call the Ipswich killer the 'Ripper' in their reports. In the case of the *Sun* it was usually the 'Suffolk Ripper', whereas the *Mirror* went with the 'Ipswich Ripper'. There is obviously a connection with two notorious serial killers from the past, Jack the Ripper and the Yorkshire Ripper, but it must be remembered why these killers got their monikers. Both of them had carried out terrible mutilations on their victims (although both had primarily attacked prostitutes, as in Ipswich) while the Ipswich killer inflicted no visible wounds at all, and certainly did not draw blood. In fact, the Ipswich killer could be noted for the sterility of his murders.

The Ipswich *Evening Star* used the headline 'Red Light Murders' in a clear reference to the town's red light district, but the fact was that the fear had spread much further than this tiny area. In a report in *The Times* on 13 December, a lecturer from Suffolk College in Ipswich, which coincidentally Gemma Adams had attended, explained the widespread feeling: 'Normally it's hard to keep the girls calm at this time of year. Usually they'd be all excitable about Christmas, partying, wanting to get away and out on the town. We were going to let the girls home early, before dark, but we've been told not to. A lot are only sixteen, and parents need to know where they are. A lot are picking them up from the bus stops.'

But the fear and media attention were only just beginning to mount. And just two days after Tania Nicol was found there was yet another tragic discovery, the third in just over a week.

CHAPTER THREE
AN EPIDEMIC OF FEAR AND PARANOIA

At 10.30am on Tuesday 7 December, the day before the body of Tania Nicol was discovered, a strange sight was observed by a passing motorist on the other side of Ipswich. Whereas both Gemma and Tania had been found to the west of Ipswich, this sighting took place to the south-east. Driving through the village of Nacton, which is about 7 miles (11.3km) from Ipswich itself, the driver saw something a short distance from the side of the road.

It was in the motorist's line of vision and he slowed down a little to take in what he had seen. It had looked like a naked figure. After a second's thought, he decided that it must have been an abandoned mannequin, the kind of shop dummy used in department stores to display clothes. This seemed to be the logical explanation and he drove on and did not report what he had seen to the police until days later.

Any other explanation must have seemed just too surreal and unbelievable.

SUNDAY, 10 DECEMBER 2006
NACTON, SUFFOLK
3.20pm

She was found in the same place by another motorist three days later. It was in an area of woodland, frosty cold in the Christmas wind, not far from the roadside, but far enough not to have been spotted by more people driving by. Like the other women, she was completely naked and exposed to the world and the elements. She lay in the undergrowth, just on the outer edge of the woods.

The motorist contacted the police immediately. It was close to the Amberfield turning and just a short distance from Amberfield School, a private school for girls. When the police arrived, they immediately cordoned off the area, in an act that must have been beginning to feel like déjà vu.

The immediate response of the police to the finding of this third body was to call it 'unexplained', a diplomatic choice of vocabulary. They were obviously concerned about public fears of there being a serial killer on the loose and so anxious to play down the links until they could be confirmed. The then Chief Constable Alistair McWhirter said that there were 'significant differences' between the new discovery and the previous two.

The officer in charge of the murder inquiry, DCS Stewart Gull, was slightly more forthcoming: 'This is a deeply disturbing development, particularly in the light of the two murder investigations which have been launched during the past fortnight. While we can't formally link the discovery of the body at Nacton with the two murders, the facts speak for themselves.'

He then went on to state the facts regarding Tania Nicol and Gemma Adams, to keep the appeals for information alive. The newly discovered body was kept at the crime scene for quite some time as thorough forensic tests were carried out. The body of the woman was finally taken to Ipswich hospital, where a Home Office pathologist conducted a post-mortem to try to establish a cause of death. It will be remembered that this had not been possible in the cases of Gemma and Tania.

The shock of the discovery of the third body was obviously huge, especially because of where the body was found. Parish Council Chairman Richard Peel told the *Sun*: 'This is shocking news. It's terrible to hear about a body being found anywhere – but it's even worse that it's next to the girls' school. I am sure it's going to be upsetting for the pupils.'

This raises the question of whether the killer knew the area well. Did the killer know that there was a girls' school so near? Did this show a sadistic streak – the need to feel power through instilling as much fear and panic as possible in the public, and especially the schoolgirls? Or was it just an opportunistic disposal site?

The third woman had yet to be formally identified and publicly named. But a distressing fact was to surface. She had not been reported missing. And this led the police and public to wonder how many other potential victims there could be out there.

The first information to be released about the identity of the third woman by the police was on the following day, Monday 11 December: 'We believe that she is a twenty-four-year-old woman who was known to work as a prostitute.' Obviously nothing further could be added until a formal identification had taken place. However, there was not long to wait. That very evening, the unfortunate woman's identity was released.

Her name was Anneli Alderton, and she had indeed been twenty-four years old. The photographs of Anneli show a pretty blonde woman whose lifestyle, which the police described as 'chaotic', had taken a toll on her appearance. The dark rings around her eyes and a somewhat strained expression betray the stress that drug abuse and general instability had brought her.

Anneli Alderton was born in Ipswich, but her childhood and young womanhood had been spent in diverse locations. Her parents, Maire and Roy, split up when she was a little girl. Anneli and her older brother Tom spent time mostly with their mother as children, but did live for a spell with their father Roy and his new wife Christine and daughter Jane. They also lived for a time in Cyprus, where their grandparents lived, when they were teenagers. Anneli's grandmother Joan Malloy said: 'She was a perfectly nice little girl and had a happy upbringing. Anni got good grades in English and Art.'

Anneli went to Copleston High School in the inner Ipswich suburb of California. She was remembered as an intelligent student and as her mother Maire told the *Sun*: 'She was a lovely bright girl. I loved her so much.' But once again the spectre of drugs moves through this story.

It seems that Anneli had been taking drugs for some time. A twenty-six-year-old prostitute and friend of Anneli told the *Sun* on 12 December: 'Anneli got into crack when she was about fourteen or fifteen. She stayed that age and never really matured. She was a vulnerable girl.' It was even reported that other girls on the streets of the Ipswich red light district referred to her as 'Crackhead Annie'.

One of the pivotal events in Anneli's life was undeniably the death of her father Roy from lung cancer in 1998. As her step-sister Jane Lowe said: 'Anneli was a very intelligent and clever girl. She was close to her dad and when he died of cancer in 1998 her world fell apart. She began mixing with the wrong crowd. She was vulnerable and eventually became a prostitute, though not through choice. One of her friends used to make a lot of money at it.'

It is a familiar picture. As Anneli's drug use escalated and began to spiral out of control, her activities as a prostitute increased too in a bid to feed her daily fix. Like most of the women working the Ipswich streets, Anneli was a contradictory mix of vulnerability and street toughness. The latter was a mask developed over time to hide the former, in order to survive in that environment.

In 2001 Anneli was living in central Ipswich in a low-level block of flats called Norwich Court. As she was the first Ipswich victim to be a mother, this made the horrible discovery doubly traumatic. As Anneli's mother Maire said on 12 December: 'I'm holding things together and trying to grieve for her as well as looking after her little one.'

Unfortunately the birth of her child did not change Anneli's way of life. In 2002, Anneli received a sentence of three-and-a-half years for street robbery, which she had no doubt committed to feed her desperate need for drugs. Anneli went to prison but did not serve the full term, being released in 2003. Her child was looked after by family members during this time.

After this Anneli and her child lived in Huddersfield, Yorkshire with Anneli's mother Maire for a time. Anneli lived in the university area of the city, while Maire and her grandchild lived in a nearby village. Anneli's grand-mother Joan Malloy lived in West Yorkshire, and when Anneli and Maire moved back to the south, Joan looked after Anneli's child. While her grandmother looked after her great-grandchild, Anneli was back in Ipswich.

Meanwhile, Anneli's mother Maire moved to Harwich in Essex and opened a small shop there with her partner. Anneli lived there as a base but often spent extended periods in nearby Colchester, where she had friends she stayed with, but no permanent address. Neighbours were to say that Anneli's visits to her mother became less frequent in the months before her death. One neighbour told the *Guardian* anonymously: 'Anneli was a very nice girl, very pretty, always dressed well. They are a very, very nice family.'

Another neighbour described Anneli as a 'very good-looking girl who dressed in skimpy clothes. She was a bit of a mad one, really. She used to come over the park with her child and could be quite intimidating to the other mums. She obviously needed some sort of help but didn't appear to be getting it.'

The fact is that by this time Anneli must have been living in her own world, one governed by drugs. As seen with both Gemma and Tania, there is little a loving parent can do when hard drugs take a firm hold. Added to this, Anneli would have been further hardened by her experiences in prison, her work on the streets and the extremely transient nature of her life.

A close friend of Anneli's mother Maire said: 'She can't believe her daughter has gone. She said to me, "How am I going to tell her child?" She was completely despairing because she didn't know how to help her daughter.'

Maire's terraced house had a Christmas 'welcome' banner hanging outside, an almost sickening reminder of the time of year, but there was nobody around in the days immediately after the tragic discovery. Anneli's child must have still been largely unaware of what was going on, but it was going to be necessary for the situation to be explained, somehow, before whispers or the television and newspaper headlines did the job.

One of the saddest aspects of Anneli's short twenty-four years was that she had been making determined efforts to get off drugs. She had attended several drug rehabilitation programmes, and while none had worked, the will to get clean for her child was there. She also had a regular boyfriend, Sam Jefford, who was twenty-one. As a fellow prostitute told the *Sun*: 'Anneli knew the other girls [Gemma and Tania]. She worked the same streets and shared clients – but I doubt they'd share regular clients. When she first got out [of prison] she was doing well. I'd heard that she'd recently been seen down the YMCA gym.'

However, in August 2006 Anneli had been arrested in Colchester after a fight outside a pub. She had allegedly attacked a police officer.

Perhaps the most telling words came from Anneli's grandmother Joan Malloy: 'The Anni I knew as a little girl had died years before. I remember her as a normal, artistic and bright little girl – happy and alive. Anneli has been a girl more sinned against than sinning, but she became addicted to heroin.'

Anneli Alderton was last seen boarding the 5.53pm train from Harwich to Colchester on Sunday 3 December, exactly a week before her body was discovered, though of course her body had been spotted earlier. The CCTV footage of this train journey would form a major part of the murder inquiry.

The lack of defence wounds on Anneli's body was strange considering that Anneli was known as a feisty woman who sometimes had a fiery temper (although her drug use also induced mood swings). As her step-sister Jane, twenty-five, said: 'She was a lovely person, but a bit of a wild child. But Anneli was tough and strong, even though she was slim, and didn't worry about the dangers of prostitution. She'd have put up a hell of a fight if anyone had attacked her.'

The sentiments and emotional reaction to the discovery of Anneli's body are distilled in an entry on the Ipswich *Evening Star*'s online condolence site, under the heading 'Pay your Tributes to Anneli': 'How can someone do this to a young girl? What did any of you do to deserve it? I can only offer my condolences to those you have left behind, watch over them from Heaven. I hope you'll be able to rest in peace and justice will be served upon the animal who made you an angel.' – Katie, Ipswich.

As public emotion rose and the panic began to set in, the police knew that they had to try to remain detached and clinical in their approach. Only cool heads would cover the ground needed to find the necessary leads. The discovery of Anneli's body had ratcheted up the pressure levels in this race against time.

The police inquiry was now really getting organised. Faced almost certainly with a serial killer or killers, the Suffolk Police knew that the hunt would take all of their resources and more. Extra resources from other forces and Scotland Yard would be forthcoming as well as leading experts in the profiling and forensic science fields. But fundamentally the public had to be protected as much as possible. The opportunities available for the killer to take another victim had to be minimised.

All three victims had worked as prostitutes, but there was no knowing if any future victims would come from a broader section of the population. The one certain factor was that the targets had all been female. Giving the population as much information and advice as possible (not a problem with the oncoming media tide) was absolutely essential. In fact, the situation was so dangerous that the police began giving cautious warnings. This tightrope between maintaining public safety and the need to prevent panic was a precarious one for those leading the investigation.

The police were now bluntly telling prostitutes to 'get off the streets' of Ipswich. These warnings were largely heeded by the women working in the red light district, where numbers fell to just a hardcore of prostitutes. It may seem incredible that any remained at all given that they were faced with an invisible killer or killers, but this illustrates just how financially desperate these sex workers were, and no doubt the need for drug money was a strong factor.

Appeals were also being made for any information about Anneli Alderton's last few days. Any sightings could well have been a crucial breakthrough. However, the last sighting remained the one of Anneli boarding the train from Harwich to Colchester on 3 December at 5.53pm, exactly a week before her body was found.

It was fortuitous that the train had CCTV cameras installed, and as soon as these were located and analysed, the police released the footage via the local and national television news, as well as on the internet. It was hoped that this segment of film might jog the memories of members of the public.

They are very moving images. It is very poignant to see Anneli Alderton alive and well so close to the time of her disappearance, and heartbreaking because of her being unaware of the tragic fate awaiting her. They cannot have been easy to watch for those who knew and loved her, but the police had to release them. They were the strongest lead the police had in relation to Anneli's murder. It is unfortunate that Anneli appears to be alone in the train carriage, as it drastically reduces the number of potential witnesses. However, this is perhaps not surprising as it was an early Sunday evening in winter on a provincial train service.

The most striking thing is how full of life she seems, like any twenty-four-year-old woman, excited and restless. She begins with her back to the camera and she is seated. Then she suddenly gets up and swings around her bag, before walking into the doorway alcove of the carriage. She checks out her reflection in the window, smiling and laughing to herself. Then she preens herself in front of the window again, has a look at her bottom over her shoulder, and pulls up her jeans. Then she sits back down in the seat, her back to the camera again. She moves her head a great deal, flicking her blonde ponytail around as she does so. Then the segment ends.

Detective Chief Superintendent Stewart Gull stressed that it was imperative that they learned where Anneli had gone when she left the train: 'We need to piece together Anneli's movements after this image was captured. At which station did Anneli get off the train? And where did she go after that? I would ask people to look carefully at the images. If anyone saw Anneli after the evening of Sunday, 3 December, we want to hear from them.'

It soon emerged that Anneli's train journey had been made to Harwich. It was a further reminder of the tragedy of Anneli's death – a young mother in the run-up to Christmas.

A further development was that Anneli was seen getting into a dark blue BMW car in Ipswich's red light district on the night she was last seen. In the following days, the national newspapers seized on this lead. On Thursday 14 December, four days after Anneli's body was found, there was a smattering of reports. The *Sun* carried an interview with an Ipswich prostitute called Lou, who was to become a regular media interviewee, both in print and on television. Lou said: 'We never saw her again. As the guy drove past with Anneli beside him, he looked towards us. He had a chubby build, glasses and short, dark hair.' The *Sun* then went on to make the rather tenuous connection that Gemma Adams had last been seen near a BMW garage.

This would have meant that after Anneli's image was captured on the train CCTV footage, she went to Ipswich to work. This is an easy journey. The small port of Harwich in Essex is south-east of Ipswich, whereas Colchester, where Anneli was then staying, lies due south of Ipswich. It would have taken a short detour north, away from the train's destination in Colchester. This was plausible, but it was never fully substantiated.

Lou described exactly what happened: 'We were all standing around eating strawberries. Anneli was alone on one side of the road, and I was on the other side of the road with two girls called Suzanne and Philly. All of a sudden, this newish dark blue BMW slowed down and went into the public car park close to Anneli. Going into the car park is a signal the driver wants a girl. Anneli went over as she was nearest. She sat in the passenger seat talking to him as he drove off. He didn't look creepy or out of the ordinary. But I have told police that this guy might have killed her and the others.' Lou added that the driver of the BMW had appeared again, four days later on 7 December on Handford Road, near the football ground.

Lou said that the working girls were not surprised when Anneli did not appear for work the next night. Apparently Anneli only worked in Ipswich three or four nights a week. DCS Stewart Gull was cautious when questioned about the BMW lead, it being one of several: 'We have spoken to the driver of a BMW as I understand it. He has not been eliminated but we have had contact with him and we may need to speak to him again.'

As with Gemma Adams and Tania Nicol, the police searched a wide area in order to try to retrieve Anneli's clothing. She was last seen wearing a black waist-length jacket with a fur-trimmed hood, a white top, blue jeans and white shoes. She was also carrying a nylon shoulder bag that was tied with cord.

There were now three separate ongoing murder inquiries, but all under the umbrella of a serial murder investigation. As well as the usual detective work, forensic and profiling angles, the police were looking into unsolved murders and disappearances going back to the early 1990s. There were also spot checks being made on vehicles seen in the red light area and questioning of the drivers. Any small point could produce a strong lead. It should be remembered that the Yorkshire Ripper Peter Sutcliffe's reign of terror was only brought to an end when he was stopped and questioned – actually in his car with a prostitute – because of false number plates on his car.

It was uncharted territory for the Suffolk Police. The scale of this investigation had never been seen before, but it was the deadly urgency that brought the most pressure. The body count was already three, and there was no telling where it would end. The Christmas period is usually one when the police are preoccupied with drunk and disorderly incidents and drink driving. But the celebrations were muted in Ipswich now. A dull gloom was in the atmosphere.

Nevertheless the police showed real commitment, vitality and professionalism in how they dealt with the gathering storm. As a local resident told this author: 'Having seen how hard the police worked, we have nothing but respect for what the Suffolk force and indeed visiting forces did. People took the mick out of it, said cor, little rural Suffolk Police force, they'll never cope. The reason why we haven't got people who can cope on their own is that this has never happened here before.'

This shocking and unwelcome phenomenon had indeed caught everyone off guard. It is hard to take in events such as these, especially as they are unfolding. Understanding abnormal events needs an examination of abnormal psychology. What could possibly make this killer or killers tick?

The fact that all three victims were prostitutes and that all were found naked immediately points to a sexual motive for the murders. But as Colin Wilson and Donald Seaman assert in their seminal book *The Serial Killers: A Study in the Psychology of Violence*: 'Serial murder is not about sex; it is about power.' The rapist too rapes to feel powerful, to be in control of another human being. After all, sex can usually be obtained by anybody who really wants or needs it, whether through a regular partner, a casual partner or a prostitute. But paying for sex is not at all emotionally or mentally stimulating for a person with power issues. There is no control involved. Such a person knows that a prostitute is only going through the motions for financial gain.

The serial murderer of course goes much further than the rapist by taking lives, but the compulsion to control is common to both. It is also worth noting that many serial rapists and serial killers have had settled relationships or access to a sexual partner, clearly indicating that sex is rarely the core motivation for such crimes.

What seems to differentiate the rapist and the serial killer from anyone else with power issues is the degree of development of violent sexual fantasy. There are many seemingly 'normal' people who have power issues, but these are generally played out mentally and emotionally only. The so-called Alpha personality is one that craves control, but thankfully mental or emotional possession or dominance is usually enough. However, when the need for dominance extends into someone's sexual fantasy life, things can become more complicated. There are of course many people who enjoy sadomasochistic practices entirely consensually, with both parties contented. But occasionally when a person's sense of power is continually thwarted in some way, and violent sexual fantasies are used to compensate, a major problem develops.

For somebody with a powerful sexual drive, external stimulants may be needed. These can take the form of pornography, role-play or the more subversive activities of peeping or flashing. The fantasist who relies on these outside stimuli to an obsessive extent may well feel ashamed and isolated by his extreme drives and needs, leading to withdrawal into a private world of fantasy. They feel safer in a world of their own making. Such a fantasist can sometimes appear perfectly ordinary to others, even close friends or family. The human mind is capable of putting life into compartments very efficiently, though this depends on whether there are other psychological disorders present or not.

Many serial killers have been very cunning and manipulative, and this is how they often manage to evade capture and claim more victims. In the case of the Ipswich murders, it seemed to be a kind of killing spree, but there was no way of knowing if the killer had committed earlier murders or not at this stage.

In this way fantasy begins to replace reality, and the fantasy is about power. When Gemma, Tania and Anneli were immobilised in some way, and then stripped naked, the killer had absolute control. It will be discussed later what might have happened between then and the dumping of the bodies, but this too would have given absolute power.

So what could push a sexual fantasist over the edge to the extreme action of serial killing? Well, if someone's reality has a lack of control these fantasies can be a great relief and give control and boost possibly low self-esteem.

There is often a deep-rooted feeling of inadequacy or inferiority within this person. Their self-image and the way they perceive their place in the world are perhaps weak and undetermined. But again, they might appear reasonably well adjusted to the outside world.

This inferiority could come from a feeling of isolation: socially, sexually or through a perceived lack of status, or a mixture of these. This powerful need for such a person to assert himself can lead to serial murder in extreme cases.

How does the serial killer develop? There is of course no single template, as we know from studies of a wide variety of convicted serial murderers, who have come from different backgrounds, had various motivations, and been of both sexes. Nevertheless the vast majority have been male, suggesting the influence of testosterone, which increases aggression. They have been of all ages, from children to elderly people. But violent fantasies have been common to all of them. A serial killer may have all or some of these following characteristics, but this should be seen as a general guide.

Childhood is when our personalities are moulded. A broken home, where parents are separated or divorced, is not a prerequisite for a serial killer, but a surprising number have come from such a background. There is often a lack of early discipline and a general feeling of instability. Sometimes there might be mental, sexual or physical abuse. Some studies suggest that many serial killers have suffered some type of brain injury, causing frontal lobe damage. The frontal lobe of the brain controls our conscious actions and if this is damaged it can lead to violent behaviour. Such a person loses his control over primitive urges and is liable to lash out.

Another early sign is that of cruelty, to animals or other children. This first foray into cruelty acts as a hardening stage and the individual becomes increasingly desensitised to inflicting and witnessing mental or physical pain, or both.

In an emotional and social sense, such future killers often display a lack of empathy and understanding of others, and an inner coldness. However, such a person might be very good at cultivating a mask to hide behind. Psychopaths are extremely good at this – think of Patricia Highsmith's character Tom Ripley – they mimic the mannerisms and reactions of others around them and present them as their own.

The fantasies themselves usually develop by the mid-teenage years, but some serial killers have had violent fantasies by the time they were seven or eight years old. Typical fantasies involve rape and murder and normally involve a submissive victim, either somebody known to the fantasist in reality or an anonymous person who has been objectified. Bondage is also common in these fantasies and the victim is at the mercy of the fantasist. In short, the latter is in complete control.

These fantasies continue to develop, becoming more and more violent. This is when the use of pornography or the more active peeping or flashing may occur. Any of these activities have elements of control: the models in pornography are objectified or become anonymous images; the peeping victim is unaware and powerless, and the flashing victim is at the complete mercy of the flasher. Any of these activities will give a temporary surge of self-esteem to the developing killer, as well perhaps as feelings of shame. This conflict might cause confusion and distress, but the fantasies will nevertheless have grown in intensity.

Moving into adulthood, the real problem starts. Up until this time, all of the crimes have usually taken place in the mind of the person. Others may have been affected in relatively minor ways, such as the victims of peeping or flashing. But these acts have as yet involved no physical contact, however disturbing they may have been to the targets.

For some these violent fantasies continue and are adequate for feeding the need for power. However, for a tiny minority the fantasies are no longer powerful enough. Whereas before the fantasy gave the developing killer a warped identity, this craving for attention and control of his environment has now become too strong. This is where fantasy becomes terrifying reality.

Most serial killers commit their first murder between their mid-twenties and early thirties. This is when the power urge can no longer be suppressed for this extreme minority. There is often a gap of years between the first and second murder as the new killer wrestles with the vestiges of any conventional conscience or fears of being caught and tries to regain control. But the urge and the exhilaration of power gained by the murder become like a drug. After the second murder the barriers really come down and the shame subsides. The killer may well know what they are doing is wrong and do everything to avoid being caught, but they are no longer living in a set of recognisable values or morals. However, they may still appear quite normal on the outside.

There are as many types of serial killer as there are psychological disorders. In the case of the Ipswich murders, there was of course no gap between the first and second murders, but then nobody knew whether the offender had committed murder before. This is why the police continued to look into the earlier unsolved murders. The profilers needed to establish a pattern in order to understand and hopefully identify the killer before more victims were claimed.

There was no telling if the Ipswich killer had some or all of these characteristics commonly found in the development of serial murderers. At the heart of the issue is the old debate about nature versus nurture. Are some people born evil, or with the capacity to commit it, again and again? Or do they become evil over time, affected by their background and circumstances, essentially victims of their environment? Most experienced clinical psychologists say that it is a mixture of both.

A further revelation was to come regarding the murder of Anneli Alderton. The post-mortem examination uncovered that Anneli had been pregnant, and this amplified the tragedy still further. It was impossible for anybody not to see the unborn child as yet another victim, and the headlines reflected this.

Anneli had been three months' pregnant and the father was her boyfriend of six months, twenty-one-year-old Sam Jefford. According to a family friend, Anneli had been very happy about expecting another baby and she had planned to tell her family soon.

Anneli's mother Maire was said to have 'howled with pain' when she was told the news of her daughter's pregnancy. The new baby would have been a little brother or sister for Anneli's child. Anneli's grandmother Joan Malloy collapsed when she heard about the murder of her unborn second grandchild.

The father, Sam Jefford, said that he would like to kill the killer himself, so deep was his sense of anger and loss.

By now the media was sharply focused on Ipswich. As well as the blanket local coverage, journalists were pouring into the town, sent by national newspapers and television stations, including the BBC and Sky News. The incredible speed of developments – three bodies discovered in eight days – brought a sense of real urgency and tension to the reporting. News was breaking daily, as police press conferences were held and appeals given out, and the media followed new avenues of inquiry. Speculation was also rife, a familiar and sometimes unhelpful trait of a manhunt of this scale.

Journalists were approaching family members and friends of Gemma, Tania and Anneli, and the overall reaction was unsurprisingly one of shock and confusion. We never expect somebody we know to become a murder victim, even if like these three women they led a more than usually risky life.

The prostitutes working in the Ipswich red light district were also frequent interviewees, in a direct effort to give the readers and viewers a glimpse into the subculture in which the three women had worked. This precarious yet ultimately banal world seems like a different planet when viewed from the outside, especially by those with no connection to Ipswich. Almost every town and city has such a subculture, but while it may be only a street away, we rarely get to see inside it. We have no direct involvement and that is how most people want it. But as a media story it is darkly fascinating, if disturbing.

The local reaction was in fact very open-minded. A native of Ipswich told this author: 'Everywhere you went – the post office, the butchers, anywhere – people were muttering about it. And I never heard anyone anywhere say anything bad about the girls. If that had happened in a major city, it's a dangerous assumption, but somebody somewhere would have said, "It doesn't matter, they're only tarts".'

The finding of a third body had hardened the resolve of the Ipswich people. The collective view was not that the victims were prostitutes and that there was therefore no need to worry. Most local residents saw it as a personal attack on their town, an affront to their community. Christmas is a time when the community is usually drawn closer together in mutual celebration and a real feeling of belonging surfaces. The shadow of evil had darkened and threatened this relaxed and welcoming atmosphere, but not totally destroyed it. Strangely, although somewhat subdued, fearful and reflective, the Ipswich community bonded together against this attack. The strength of individuals and a community is only tested in adversity and Ipswich was not found lacking.

The sense of fear was indeed rising. With the killer still at large, there was no telling who would be the next victim and whether women not working in the red light district could also be targeted. The police were issuing regular warnings for everybody to be extra vigilant, especially females. This resulted in some success in the red light district, where prostitute numbers had radically reduced.

Police patrols had been stepped up, and the warnings from the police via the media were getting through.

The natural build-up of fear in the community was also a major factor, of course. Confusion brings fear and a lack of control, and such an invisible menace can only be tackled by safety precautions. Nevertheless, a handful of prostitutes were still working the very streets where the three victims had worked, and some of them knew Gemma, Tania and Anneli well. The desperation for money is very apparent when taking such risks.

Amongst the wider female population, the trepidation was also spreading. As in the Yorkshire Ripper manhunt a quarter of a century earlier, no woman felt safe in Ipswich at night by this time. The police advised women to go out in pairs or groups as much as possible. A local wine merchant told this author: 'I think the town was justifiably jumpy. I can give you one example – a restaurant in the town, on a Saturday before Christmas, cancelled their wine order. The restaurant owner said that his restaurant only seats thirty-five or forty, and that an office party of seventeen had cancelled, as the girls didn't dare come into Ipswich.'

The provincial and calm air of the town was now heavy with apprehension. A town whose local council had periodically tried to market it as a bright and personable 'young' place, using the term 'Hipswich' to attract fashionable youth, now found itself dealing with a national and soon international image tainted by serial murder. Logically we know that it could happen anywhere, but at the time it seemed that Ipswich was fated to live in shadow.

The pace of the macabre events was largely the cause of this feeling. Nobody had time to take in and attempt to rationalise the terrible events. On their very front lawn a terrifying situation was unfolding, and nobody knew when and how it would stop. The fear of the unknown and the fear of darkness are tightly entwined. During daylight, as people did their best to go about their business as usual, it was possible to momentarily forget the evil in their midst. But then an overheard conversation, a headline displayed on a newspaper, an appeal poster or a newsflash, would bring it all back. There was no real escape.

The time of year was also a decisive factor. The murders had occurred just as schools were about to close for Christmas and offices shut for the holiday period. A time for letting down hair and dropping reserve had coincided with a need to be suspicious, careful and tentative. Hedonism was being replaced by hesitation.

The feelings of sympathy for Gemma and Tania had been heartfelt but muted in the local community. But when Anneli's body was found, the realisation that a killer or killers were preying on the town was beginning to dawn. The two days between Tania and Anneli being discovered saw a shift in local consciousness. People began to empathise with the three women, no matter how removed from the everyday their lives had been at the time of their deaths. This mixture of compassion and fear would only grow over the coming days. Both feelings were intensely real. The compassion was for three women who had hurt nobody, but had had their futures taken away. The fact that Anneli had been pregnant heightened this feeling further.

So the effects of the sequence of events went much further than the trauma suffered by the families and friends of the victims. The whole community was beginning to be deeply affected. The fact that the inquiry was now making the front pages of national newspapers and the main television news bulletins meant that people who had never visited Ipswich and knew its name largely through the football team and the odd media story, were now surrounded by the town daily, as the twenty-first century media spread the news.

For the people of Ipswich itself, it was a nightmare they hoped would pass, or that they would suddenly wake up from. It truly was the nightmare before Christmas. And it was not difficult to imagine what most of the Ipswich people wanted for Christmas. They wanted to be delivered from this evil.

The media publicity and police appeals had resulted in many calls from the public. The vast majority were made up of snippets of information from local people. All of these had to be sifted and assimilated and then formed into as cohesive a pattern as possible. As Suffolk Assistant Chief Constable Jacqui Cheer said: 'A good way to describe the progress we are making would be to compare the investigation to a jigsaw. We have constructed the edges, now we have to fill in the middle.'

As well as the hunt for the killer it was also imperative that any missing women or girls in the area were traced as soon as possible. They were all potential victims, and with bodies being uncovered so quickly, there was no way of knowing who would be next or if anybody else had already been murdered in this spree. There were two women in particular who were causing great concern; both of them were prostitutes who worked in Ipswich's red light district.

The two women were Annette Nicholls, aged twenty-nine, and Paula Clennell, twenty-four. Annette had last been seen just before 10pm on Tuesday 5 December in Norwich Road, Ipswich, and Paula was last sighted at around 1am in Rendlesham Court, Ipswich, on the same day that Anneli's body had been discovered, Sunday, 10 December. Both women had vanished during the eight-day period when the three victims were found.

Detective Chief Superintendent Stewart Gull said: 'Both of these girls were reported missing as a result of publicity generated by the inquiries into the murders of Gemma Adams and Tania Nicol. In the current climate, we are concerned for their welfare and are making urgent inquiries to locate them. I would ask the girls themselves or anyone with information as to their whereabouts to contact police immediately.'

Annette Nicholls was described as 5ft 3in (1.60m) tall, with a slim build and brown, shoulder-length hair. Paula was 5ft 7in (1.70m) tall, with a medium build and mousey, shoulder-length hair.

This information was given at the same time as an appeal for information regarding Gemma, Tania and Anneli. It was obvious to everyone that the police were very apprehensive as to the safety of Annette and Paula.

DCS Gull then spoke directly to the killer: 'Make contact with Suffolk Police. You have a significant problem. Give me a call and we can deal with this.'

DCS Gull then said that a number of 'interesting individuals' were being looked into, and that while the events were challenging, the Suffolk Police were coping. Offers of help had been accepted from the Norfolk, Hampshire and Cambridgeshire police forces. 'We have three senior detectives leading the inquiry and over one hundred staff work on all three cases. It's testing, but it is what we do.'

DCS Gull then spoke directly to the killer again: 'My appeal is simple. Give yourself up.'

On the morning of Tuesday 12 December, the post-mortem results on Anneli Alderton were released. No definitive cause of death had been ascertained for Gemma Adams or Tania Nicol. But this time it was different. Anneli Alderton had been asphyxiated.

The medical definition of asphyxia, as given by the Hutchinson Encyclopedia, is as follows: 'Suffocation; a lack of oxygen that produces a potentially lethal build-up of carbon dioxide waste in the tissues. Asphyxia may arise from any one of a number of causes, including inhalation of smoke or poisonous gases, obstruction of the windpipe (by water, food, vomit, or a foreign object), strangulation, or smothering. If it is not quickly relieved, brain damage or death ensues.'

There were no more details given by the police as to the exact cause of the asphyxia that had killed Anneli at this stage. But it did help to explain why there were no defensive wounds on her body. A young, feisty woman such as Anneli would surely have done everything in her power to defend herself against a murderous attack. There should have been either bruises, scratches or cuts on her hands and forearms, or a degree of bruising to her face or torso, if the killer had been forced to silence her quickly. So had she been in some way incapacitated? Or had she been asphyxiated immediately?

She could have been incapacitated by being drugged or gassed. If she had been asphyxiated immediately, it inevitably leads to the conclusion that any acts done to her were performed post-mortem, or after death.

But there were also no signs of sexual assault on Anneli and there had not been any on Gemma or Tania either. This leads to several theories as to why the killer committed murder and these will be discussed later.

If Anneli had been smothered with a cloth (perhaps itself covered in chloroform), this would help explain why there were no defensive wounds. She may have had no warning of the attack. She might even have been partially or fully clothed and then stripped after death.

If the cause of death were manual strangulation, using either bare hands around the neck or a ligature of some kind, then this fits the profile of a serial killer discussed earlier, who murders for power and control. Strangulation is about as personal as murder gets. It involves close personal contact and brute force. No doubt the killer got excitement from this power.

As Brian Masters writes in his book *The Shrine of Jeffrey Dahmer*, this is the ultimate method of killing for the sadistic power killer. Dahmer killed many men using this method. As Masters says:

'Strangulation as a method of killing offers a more tantalising opportunity for control than any other, the victim being wholly at the mercy of the amount of pressure the murderer chooses to exert. It may take five minutes to squeeze the life out of someone, but that time can be prolonged by the diminution of pressure and its gradual re-imposition. In such a circumstance, the murderer is in total control of life and death – he can grant life to the victim as well as dispatch him [or her] into the afterworld.'

What could be certain at this stage was that the Ipswich killer liked close contact with the victims. So why had there been no signs of asphyxia on Gemma Adams or Tania Nicol? And no signs of sexual assault on all three women? The finding of asphyxiation as Anneli Alderton's cause of death threw up as many questions as it answered, especially in relation to the other two victims. But at least there was finally a definitive cause of death.

The police were also waiting for toxicology results on all three women, and this could take up to six weeks. If they had been drugged or gassed, this would show up and would help elucidate the modus operandi of the Ipswich killer and, in turn, personality, background and motivations.

Anneli's family, the police and the public had little time to digest and ponder all these new questions. The media had barely released all this information when something happened. Within hours, there would be further shocks, the biggest yet.

CHAPTER FOUR
THE TERROR, THE TERROR

TUESDAY, 12 DECEMBER 2006
LEVINGTON, SUFFOLK
3.05pm

It was mid-afternoon when the police received a telephone call from a member of the public. The man had been walking along a lay-by just off the Old Felixstowe Road near the village of Levington. This is just over a mile (1.6km) south-east of Nacton, where Anneli Alderton's body had been discovered two days earlier. As he walked along, he had seen the naked body of a woman about 20ft (6.1m) from the road.

Within minutes a police helicopter was flying to the scene; another team rushed by road. The police were by now becoming accustomed to this unusual routine. The sense of dread and fatalism that must have gripped the minds of the officers in those minutes as they made their way to this fourth murder site in ten days can only be imagined. But their professionalism kicked in – they had a job to do, as individuals and as a team.

The woman's body was located in woodland but incredibly close to a busy road. It seemed that the killer was playing some kind of game, perhaps taunting the police and the public, so little effort had been made to conceal the body. There was also no water around, just as in Anneli's case. This increasing lack of care taken by the killer in the disposal of victims also meant that there was more chance of forensic clues and particularly DNA evidence however. The killer or killers were either becoming increasingly complacent or just did not care any more.

While the helicopter hovered in the sky above the woodland, the team on the ground set to work. The area was immediately cordoned off. In close proximity to the A14 road, it was necessary to preserve the crime scene as much as possible. The peaceful village of Levington would never be the same again. The local pub, the village church and the green area in the centre where the village comes together for fetes and gatherings were all now tainted. Close by, a young woman had been dumped with no mercy. The dream of a peaceful English countryside was shattered.

3.45pm
The police team was continuing its search for clues in the area immediately around the woman's body. The fields around were static, just the wildlife carrying on as normal, oblivious to the evil in its midst, or perhaps just accepting of human nature, animal as it is at its basest level.

It was then that one of the helicopter crew pinpointed something on the ground. Confirmation was needed for what had been seen. A closer inspection brought the truth that no-one wanted to discover: there was a second body.

She was found just a couple of hundred metres away, and like the other bodies she was also naked. No more care had been taken in her disposal. The police requested more officers and they were soon deployed to the scene. The shock was only overcome by action.

DCS Stewart Gull made a statement swiftly, knowing that the media would soon be onto this. He said: 'Because of the discovery of two further bodies close to where the body of Anneli Alderton was found, we can only fear the worst. The natural assumption is that these are the bodies of the two missing women Annette Nicholls and Paula Clennell.'

The families of the two women were informed though as yet there was no formal identification. In fact, the first woman's body was not removed from the site until the following day, and the second woman not moved until 14 December. On that same day the first body was identified as Paula Clennell, twenty-four. On 15 December, it was confirmed that the second body was that of Annette Nicholls, aged twenty-five at the time of her death.

A detailed forensic examination was then carried out in the woodland area. The lower branches of trees, the woodland floor and hedges were searched for any clothing or personal items belonging to the two women. Police officers formed lines to search the area and a surrounding radius with a centimetre by centimetre scrutiny. The smallest clue could provide a lead. The ground was checked for footprints and tyre tracks that would be highly significant.

There was nothing left now at the site of the two women's bodies – just two indentations where they had been. Both had worked as prostitutes in Ipswich's red light district, about 5 miles (8km) from the broken peace of Levington. Like the first three victims, Paula and Annette had both been drug addicts and led risky lives. But their lives should never have ended as they did and the deep sense of double tragedy just thirteen days before Christmas was almost unfathomable.

It was soon revealed that Paula Clennell had given an interview to Anglia Television news, an interview that was later syndicated nationally through the ITV network. The interview was given on Tuesday, 5 December, exactly a week before her body was found at Levington, and five days before she was last seen.

Interviewed on the streets of Ipswich in the days after the discovery of Gemma Adams' body, she gave her thoughts on the climate of fear amongst prostitutes in the town. Paula said that she felt sick about the murder of Gemma but that she had to keep working the streets as she 'needed the money'. She then went on to say: 'It would be safer to get a flat and work from there, but it's getting a flat that's the problem.'

Paula admitted that she had had a couple of 'nasty experiences' working as a prostitute, but that she had carried on. But she added that since Gemma's murder, she was much more worried about getting into cars, and that the police presence had reduced the number of her clients.

At the end of the interview, Paula reportedly walked back in the direction of the red light district.

Paula Clennell was last seen on Sunday 10 December, when she left a friend's house in Ipswich riding a bike.

Later that same day Paula phoned a friend, saying that she needed somewhere to stay. Her family formally reported her missing on Monday 11 December in response to the growing publicity about the Ipswich murders. Her body was found the next day.

But until her body was formally identified, her parents, Brian, fifty-seven, and Isabella, forty-seven, refused to give up hope of their daughter being found alive. Brian Clennell told the *Sun*: 'I have never been one for God, but I will be down on my knees tonight praying that my daughter is still alive. Don't ever tell me there's no hope. There's always hope until the police tell me otherwise.'

Brian and Isabella Clennell divorced in the mid-1990s. Isabella, Paula and her older sister Alice relocated to Norwich, while Brian stayed in Berwick-upon-Tweed, Northumberland. Her father Brian had no idea that Paula was a prostitute. When he found out, it was a shock: 'The first I heard about Paula being missing was through the news. It has only been in the last two days [11-12 December] that I have discovered about the life Paula was living. I can only assume she was driven to it out of pure desperation. I hate to hear mention of the words "Paula Clennell" and "prostitute" in the news.'

It was during this period of waiting, between Paula being reported missing and her body found, that Brian Clennell had made an emotional appeal to Paula to make contact: 'We all love you, there's nothing to hide, everyone loves you. Please make a call to me, or your niece and your nephews, and just say that you're alive.'

The shock of discovering that his daughter had been working as a prostitute was too much for Mr Clennell at this raw and uncertain time: 'I must send out my heart to the families of those identified in this horrific, perverted, psycho, sicko campaign. This man needs to be caught, and I think the truth lies with the punters. The fat, smelly perverts. They should come forward and stop this murder that's going on.'

Mr Clennell had last heard from Paula by a letter in which she had asked to borrow £15 from him. He had sent her the money to an address in Ipswich. Her mother Isabella also last heard from Paula by letter on 24 November. Paula had written that she was going to do the Christmas shopping soon and that she wanted to meet in town before Christmas.

When the first Levington body was formally identified as Paula, Brian Clennell was understandably full of rage. He told the *Sun*: 'This bastard has to be caught. What sort of person does this? This person must be walking around the streets like one of us, but he is not – he's isn't human.'

Paula's father then went on to imply that Paula might have been killed because she was a prostitute. This 'hatred of prostitutes' theory will be discussed later. Mr Clennell said: 'He may see them as evil because of what they do, but he is the evil one. This animal will strike again.'

Paula was a pretty young woman with reddish-mousey hair and a pale complexion. The photographs of her show a well-proportioned face with delicate features and a mouth that could easily break into a smile. She was a curious mixture of sweetness and shrewdness, a sort of knowing Cupid. Her way of life and environment no doubt gave her a streetwise edge, but, like Anneli Alderton, under this she was a vulnerable woman.

Her early years were stable and loving, and after she moved to Norwich with her mother and sister following her parents' split, she continued to be a well-rounded girl. At the age of sixteen she was publicly commended and her photograph appeared in the local paper when she helped a pensioner who had fallen over and hurt herself. Soon after this Paula moved out of home to live with friends. Within a year, however, she was regularly using heroin, and this addiction finally led to prostitution to fund the habit. Her father Brian was sure that she fell in with the wrong crowd after moving to Ipswich.

Paula was the mother of three children, but all three were taken away one by one by social services when her heroin addiction was discovered. They were placed into care and Paula never got over their loss. The youngest one had been ill just before being taken into care and Paula had visited the child in hospital. Paula left a card at the hospital which read 'My heart beats every beat for you.' The little child had been living with the mother of the father. A few weeks after leaving hospital, the last child that Paula had access to was taken into care too.

In an interview with *The Sun* it was said that Paula earned up to three hundred pounds a day as a prostitute but that most of it went on drugs.

Paula's mother Isabella said that Paula had become depressed after the birth of her first child and that this had led her into drugs, changing her life irrevocably. Paula had maintained contact with her sister Alice too, who has children of her own. Paula had recently told her mother that she was terrified of working the streets, but that she wanted money to buy a flat or a house so that she could fight to get her three children back. The police were to confirm that Paula led a transient existence with no fixed address.

But at one stage she had stayed in one place for five months. A friend of Paula, an ex-soldier called Brian Wilmshurst, had taken her in and let her live in his house for that period. He told Sky News: 'I think because I never abused her, hit her or swore, she felt safe and secure here.' He said that their relationship had been platonic, just one friend helping another. He was also enlightening about Paula's character, which had obviously been hardened by her addiction and environment: 'She was a thief, a bit of a magpie. She's like a cat: very feline, affectionate, loyal, but not loyal at all – that's Paula.'

Mr Wilmshurst, fifty-one, also said that Paula was very sharp and 'on the ball' and that he would never have believed that she would become the victim of a serial killer. 'It must have been someone she knew,' he said. The last time he had seen her was about six weeks before her body was found and she had visibly deteriorated since the time she had stayed with him. Mr Wilmshurst said: 'She was dirty, smelly, scruffy and spotty. Somewhere along the line she went really rotten.'

When Paula was last seen on Sunday 10 December, she was wearing a navy blue anorak with a horizontal light blue band across the chest and one sleeve, a grey top with a hood, light-coloured jeans with a pattern on the pockets, and Reebok classic trainers with a navy blue and light blue-grey flash. After leaving her friend's home at Rendelsham Court in Ipswich, off the Handford Road and close to the junction with Burlington Road (in the north-west of Ipswich town centre), it was impossible to trace her. There was the phone call to a friend later, but that was it. Was Paula aware of the discovery of Anelli Alderton's body that very afternoon?

Paula's father remembered her as 'mischievous, but a wonderful person. She loved children, she loved pets. She was a loving, kind daughter'. But there was little doubt that drugs had changed Paula, as they had all the Ipswich victims. They led her into prostitution and to losing her three children.

Paula Clennell apparently always thought that she would die before her twenty-fifth birthday. She had a sort of premonition that she would die young. Tragically she was proved right: when she died she was just twenty-four years of age.

Annette Nicholls was the woman whose body was also found at Levington, close to Paula Clennell's body and discovered just afterwards. Annette had worked as a prostitute in the Ipswich red light district too. At the age of twenty-nine, she was the oldest of the five victims.

Annette was reported missing on Monday 11 December, the day before her body was found. She had not been seen since 9.50pm on Tuesday 5 December, on Norwich Road in Ipswich, exactly a week before her body was found. Like Paula, she was reported missing as a result of the escalating publicity surrounding the murders.

Annette was a beautiful woman with a bright smile that brought out dimples in her cheeks. Her long dark brown hair was parted in the middle and fell down below her shoulders. She was nicknamed 'Netty' by her friends and she seemed to be a very personable young woman. Unfortunately, as with all the Ipswich victims, the fatal influence of hard drugs haunted her for the last years of her short life.

In an interview with the *Guardian*, Annette's cousin Tanya Nicholls said: 'She used to be an absolutely outstanding person with the most lovely personality.' Annette was also a mother whose child had been the focus of her life. Rosemary was hit extremely hard by the loss of her daughter and her grandchild's mother. The police did their best to console her but there could be little lasting comfort for such a cruel loss.

Annette had been a very loving and carefree girl with lots of friends. She always enjoyed fashion and cosmetics and when she was twenty-one she enrolled on a course in beauty therapy at Suffolk College, where Gemma Adams had also studied. The course lasted four years and when she completed it in 2002 her future looked very positive. Annette had a real passion for beauty treatments and she would visit the homes of friends, offering beauty tips and giving different treatments. But around a year after leaving college, drugs began to take a firm hold on her.

Annette's cousin Tanya, thirty-seven, said to the *Sun*: 'Almost overnight she got into heroin and it changed her, like flicking a light switch. She used to be such a together person. She was a brilliant mother. Her house was immaculate. We basically just lost her.'

There was certainly a marked change in Annette's lifestyle. From a smiling, positive young woman looking forward to a career as a beautician, she had become a drug addict forced to sell herself to feed her habit.

However, it was not completely negative. Annette had left her semi-detached council house and moved on to the new upmarket Ravenwood estate in Ipswich, sharing her new home with a man. An old neighbour from the council estate said that Annette was 'really lovely' and that she had not been working as a prostitute when she lived there.

But Annette and her male friend did not keep up the payments on the new house and it was repossessed about a month before her body was found. Annette was living in bed and breakfast hostels at the time of her disappearance.

Her cousin Tanya last saw Annette about three weeks before she disappeared; Annette was working on the streets. Tanya told the *Sun*: 'I just wish I'd picked her up and dragged her home. It's awful to think what's happened to her.'

Annette's other uncle, Peter, who was fighting prostate cancer at the time her body was found, said: 'I thought the world of her. I was devastated when I heard what she was doing. The last time I saw her she promised me she was off drugs.' He helped to search woodland on 12 December, but not the spot where his niece and Paula were found. He added: 'I'm so glad I didn't go there... I would have found them.'

It seems that Annette was very fearful about the predatory killer in her midst, one of whose victims had already been found when she vanished. But she did not stop working. However, she was taking some precautions. A friend of Annette, who wanted to remain anonymous, had spoken to her the day before she disappeared. She had told him that she was not going to accept any work from new clients as it was too dangerous. He said: 'Annette said she was freaking out about the other girls disappearing. She was using her mobile to call her regular clients. So I'm convinced she knew her killer.'

This does sound plausible; if all of the women had known their killer as a regular punter or a 'face', it would explain how they could be lured away so easily. Whatever really did happen, it seems that Annette was wary of strangers at this time and so surely would have been extra cautious.

Yet another short life had been brutally cut off. Another family was left to face a traumatic Christmas and New Year. For the police, a fifth victim had been found in ten days. Would there be any more? When? Where?

The tragic double discoveries of 12 December were shocking to everybody in the country and further afield. The Suffolk Police had to pick up any pieces they could, fit them together and run with the leads. But they were stunned. Detective Chief Superintendent Stewart Gull admitted that his officers were 'emotionally overwhelmed' by the sheer scale of the terrible events.

It was the speed of developments as much as anything that was hard to deal with. There was no real time to process what had happened, emotionally and mentally. Not that any of it was easy to rationalise. But the police more than anyone were exposed to this maelstrom. They were on the front line, feeling the pressure of an invisible predator or predators, not knowing when any of it would stop.

Between 11 and 14 December, around 2,500 calls were received from the public, offering information and any help they could. All of these had to be sifted through, the useful filtered from the useless, with any possible leads or suspects followed up. Police from other forces had now arrived in Ipswich, giving DCS Gull a team of one hundred and fifty officers.

The police were also in contact with American police in Atlantic City, as a large-scale investigation was also taking place there into a sequence of four prostitute murders: sharing and pooling of information in such similar cases could potentially lead to procedural pointers on both sides. This pragmatism on the part of DCS Gull's team was a signal of just how wide-ranging their inquiry was.

Police helicopters were passing over the Ipswich area during daylight hours, criss-crossing the sky in the hope of seeing something. Nobody wanted to find another victim, but this task had to be undertaken. There was also the matter of the clothes of the victims. If they were found they could give some clues: on top of the location where they were found, they might also hold DNA evidence or hairs and fibres. Whilst all of the five victims were found completely naked, some of them were still wearing jewellery. Some killers would have taken this as a trophy, a souvenir of their depraved power. But the Ipswich killer seemed to show no interest in this.

Comparisons with the Yorkshire Ripper, Peter Sutcliffe, were constantly being made. But Sutcliffe had committed his murders over years, not weeks. As the then Chief Constable of Suffolk Police, Alistair McWhirter said: 'No one has had to deal with this before. If you think of the Yorkshire Ripper, the murders took place over a long period of time.'

This is undoubtedly true. No British police force has ever been so stretched and put under so much pressure for a swift result (due to public safety) in modern times. There have been huge murder cases – the Moors murders, the case of Dr Harold Shipman, the Soham murders, to name just a few. But these investigations were more focused in nature. The closest to the Ipswich murder manhunt must be the Yorkshire Ripper inquiry, with the sheer terror on the streets and the huge burden placed on the police. The ripper did kill many victims, but over a six-year period.

The Suffolk Police had found five bodies in ten days and opened five massive murder inquiries. True, technology has improved enormously since the Yorkshire Ripper inquiry, especially in the computer systems for police records and with the forensic leaps of the last three decades, but the speed was the biggest hurdle. No police force could be perfectly prepared for such an eruption of evil.

All five victims worked as prostitutes in the Ipswich red light district. All five were heroin addicts. Three were mothers. All were found naked in rural locations. None had defence wounds. None had died where they were found.

The police had to try to find some common links. Regular clients, drug dealers, friends and anyone suspicious had to be interviewed and either crossed off the list of possible suspects or followed up.

The speed of the events has to be put into perspective, however. Although all five victims had been found between 2 and 12 December, the police had in fact to investigate a six-week period. Tania had gone missing on 30 October, around six weeks before 12 December. This only increased the volume of legwork, with many more leads needing investigation.

One of the key areas in which the police officers, forensic experts and profilers had to consider thoroughly was the idea of the 'storage' of the bodies. If none of the women had died where they were found, they must have been kept somewhere first. It was almost certain that they were killed, stored and finally dumped under the cover of darkness.

The first two victims found, Gemma Adams and Tania Nicol, had been left to the west of Ipswich, not far apart geographically. Both were found in water. Anneli Alderton was found just a relatively short distance from Paula Clennell and Annette Nicholls, the latter two being found very close together. The final three were left to the east of Ipswich, and not in water – they were dumped in woodland not far from the roadside.

If the killer was dumping the bodies in fairly remote areas, there must have been a vehicle used – a car, a van or a lorry. This would be a very important factor if and when a suspect was arrested. Even if a vehicle has been cleaned well, microscopic forensic evidence can still be found.

The 'storage theory' was one that preoccupied the police. The premises used for this purpose would obviously be a major police target and a good comprehension of the killer or killers' modus operandi could only help bring the manhunt to a speedier close. A detailed profile of the predator, an understanding of the abnormal psychology at work and possible motives and reasoning were all key to the inquiry.

As a police source told the media at the time: 'It seems inconceivable that the killer is targeting two girls and snatching them at the same time. With regard to the latest bodies, it seems likely that he killed one, kept her somewhere, then killed the second before disposing of them together. The bodies of the first two victims were found 2 miles [3.2km] apart in the same brook but we cannot rule out the possibility they were dumped together and water carried one away.'

This was a key question. Were Gemma Adams and Tania Nicol dumped together or were they left separately in the locations where they were found? If they were dumped in the same place and water currents moved one of the bodies downstream, were they disposed of at the same time? Or did the killer return to the dumping site with another victim?

The police source continued: 'This man is killing and disposing of bodies in a very organised way, almost certainly under cover of darkness. But he does not appear to be making any great attempts at concealing the bodies, particularly in the last three instances.'

The psychology of the body disposal pattern will be discussed later, but it is important to emphasise that what happened to the girls between being taken and dumped was absolutely crucial to the progress of the inquiry.

The police were also following up their investigations into earlier unsolved murders of young women in a wide radius of Ipswich. On 13 December, detectives went to see the mother of Natalie Pearman, a sixteen-year-old prostitute who was found strangled in Norwich in 1992. Nobody had ever been convicted of this murder fourteen years earlier, but the police had to tell Natalie's mother Lin that they were not linking her daughter's murder with the Ipswich inquiry at this time.

It was also soon revealed that Annette Nicholls had been seen getting into a dark blue BMW by the owner of a local shop. A security guard was also reported to have seen a BMW in the area. This was a link that was threading through the manhunt, as it will be remembered that Anneli Alderton was also seen getting into a BMW before she disappeared.

The sighting of Annette was on Fore Street, a road on the east side of Ipswich town centre, and she had been seen being picked up outside a public phone box and then dropped back five minutes later. It was said that the BMW could have been a 5 Series with shiny alloy wheels, perhaps driven by a white man in his forties, wearing a business suit. The police continued to play down this BMW thread but were paying it close attention.

The locals of Ipswich, particularly in the red light district, were helping the police in their urgent enquiries by reporting anything suspicious. There were many such reports, as there always are when the public are nervous and anxious to help. Most turned out to have mundane explanations. One example is of a man who was seen trying to exit a car park at speed, firing the engine and then reversing. A registration was taken and given to the police by a local man. The police knew that such snippets of information had to be followed up, as any tiny piece of information might lead to a breakthrough.

By 15 December the police revealed that they were looking at five key suspects. No firm details of these suspects were released at this stage for obvious reasons, but it was certainly encouraging that a nucleus of informed suspicion was forming in the inquiry.

As reported in the *Sun*, a friend of both Tania Nicol and Annette Nicholls had come forward, giving the police three leads for suspects. But these were not among the five key suspects. Jack, a fifty-year-old factory worker, supplied the police with information about a 'dogger', a businessman and a taxi driver.

The term 'dogging' is a relatively new one used to describe the phenomenon of people having sex in open, public places where there is a risk of being seen; the strangers who go to such sites to watch also sometimes join in. Anneli Alderton had been found in Nacton on 10 December just half a mile (0.8km) from a known 'dogging' site. The man described as a dogger by Jack was wealthy, known widely among Ipswich prostitutes, owned a boat and lived near the coast. He was a long-time client of Tania Nicol.

The taxi driver was a man who was also a repeat client of Tania Nicol. During their times together he would ask her to perform a role-play in which she pretended to be a passenger in his taxi; unable to pay the fare, she would have sex with him in lieu of payment. But at the end *he* would always pay *her*.

The businessman took Tania shopping on Sundays sometimes, especially to the Bluewater shopping centre in Kent. He had once bought her some gold stilettos and possibly, it was alleged, the pink stiletto shoes she had been wearing when she disappeared.

This is just a flavour of the avenues that the inquiry was taking outside of the strongest suspects. In addition to this the police were using radio cars and ANPR (Automatic Number Plate Recognition) to track anyone seen repeatedly in the red light district. These would then be put into the national police database to provide a rapid cross-reference.

The warnings to prostitutes in Ipswich to stay off the streets were reported again and again. The Deputy Chief Constable, Jacqui Cheer, even went so far as making her personal mobile phone number public so that prostitutes could call her directly if they had any information or were frightened. This was unprecedented. DCC Cheer said: 'My personal message to working girls is simple – please stay off the streets. If you're out alone at night, you're putting yourself in danger.'

The events of 12 December and the accumulated effect of the discovery of five victims so far had lent a new even sharper energy and tension to the police investigation. The clock felt as if it was racing, and the media interest in the murders was reaching fever pitch.

A story such as the Ipswich murders that keeps running day by day and builds in tension was bound to attract huge media focus. After the two further bodies were discovered on 12 December it turned into something of a feeding frenzy. Every major newspaper and television station was getting in on the action. Print and television journalists and broadcasters, along with the accompanying technical crews, were pouring into the town. What had begun as a trickle was developing into a flood.

And like an earthquake tremor, the vibrations were reaching further afield. First it was a local news story, and then national, and now international interest was building. Journalists from as far as the other side of Europe, the United States and Japan were coming to town. Added to this were the syndication rights offered by news agencies and the internet; the latter especially allowed any developments to be reported in real time.

There is a saying in journalism – 'If it bleeds, it leads'. Any story that involves violence or death is of massive media interest. Such stories are of vital human interest – anything that threatens life itself seems to appeal to the human psyche. The details of the stories might be disturbing and the fear generated real, but we are nonetheless deeply fascinated by it. The Ipswich murders were a classic human interest story.

The national newspapers in particular sent teams of journalists to cover the story. They were approaching everybody, from the families of the victims, to prostitutes, to ordinary local residents. The television stations were also taking it very seriously. The BBC began to send major news anchormen and women to Ipswich for outside broadcasts. What had begun as a local news item was now dominating the front pages of major newspapers and the main news bulletins.

The time of year definitely had an impact on the scope of the story. Christmas is not the time of year when we expect to be reading, watching and thinking about acts of evil. And Ipswich was not an obvious place for this to happen. A fairly low-profile town with a provincial atmosphere just did not seem right. The urban and moral decay of the modern city where the pace is fast and communication between people more muted would not have been so shocking. The Suffolk countryside surrounding Ipswich was not stained with blood but by notoriety and fear.

Of course the media does have a duty to keep the public informed of any danger. Nevertheless it is fair to say that some of the reporting on the Ipswich murders was somewhat wide of the remit of public information. One local resident told this author: 'These girls were human beings and Ipswich pretty much stood up and said that, amongst itself, and to the sleazy London press who came here looking for a bad angle.'

When a story like this is running, every newspaper, especially the tabloids, wants to beat the others to the scoop, and this can only be done by news gathering. It is not surprising that some Ipswich locals were shocked by this invasion, especially with the way some newspapers referred to the victims and specifically with the way their prostitution and drug addictions were reported.

In the following days, many of the national newspapers ran psychological profiles along with comments from leading clinical psychologists and crime writers. Sometimes they went one stage further and one paper even named a man who allegedly had a mission to get prostitutes off the streets and had reportedly been a friend of the victims. This man, a property developer, eventually had to give an interview to deny that he was 'the fat man in the BMW'. He said: 'I drive a Land Rover Freelander' in an interview with the Ipswich *Evening Star*.

One thing was certain – the media presence in Ipswich would only increase in the coming days. Detective Chief Superintendent Gull only formally confirmed that the police were looking for a serial killer on 15 December. In reality everybody knew this already, but the announcement made it official and media interest would only escalate.

The arrival of journalists and outside broadcast and catering vans did have an effect on the local population, as well as on the wider view of the town as seen from the outside. But the primary effect was fear, which the police were desperate to prevent turning to panic.

The air of muted terror in Ipswich that was mounting by the day was tempered by a feeling of mystery. Nobody knew which direction to look in, quite what to expect next. The feeling of awareness that an evil killer or killers were in the midst of the locals was an unsettling one. As a local man told this author: 'You first wonder if he's one of the usual street faces you see walking past or not. Can we identify him – are we actually close enough to a mass murderer so that we know what he looks like?'

There was no way of knowing if the killer lived locally but the evidence did seem to point that way. The way that the bodies were dumped around a radius of the town implied in many people's minds that the killer knew the area well. But what would he or they look like?

It was the talk of the town. Wherever two or more people congregated it was the main or only subject of conversation. There was naturally some finger pointing and unfounded suspicions forming of the 'he looks strange' variety. This was especially true about men who lived very private lives that the community knew little or nothing about. In a climate of fear such paranoia is bound to surface. Newcomers to Ipswich and strangers also became objects of suspicion. In a big city most people live in relative anonymity, but in a provincial town differences stand out.

Also, in a town of around 120,000 people, it was common for locals to know someone who knew the family of one of the victims. The reaction to the deaths of the five unfortunate women themselves was largely compassionate and understanding. Many Ipswich residents had not previously known where the red light district was, or even that there was one at all. Likewise many did not know how many women actually worked the streets regularly. It is the nature of such subcultures to have a low profile and in Ipswich it was no different.

The main focus of fear and fevered rumour and speculation was rightly reserved for the serial killer. It was universally considered to be a man or men (although it was possible that a female could be an accomplice) but what did he or they look like? What did the killer do for a living? Had the killer just served them in a shop? Was he the bus driver who took their children to school?

Local trade was hit. The shop assistant at a hardware store in the town centre said that business had dropped off. 'People are being much more cautious,' he said. It was getting to the stage where people, especially young women, were only going out if they had to.

The use of taxis was also in decline in those dark days. Richard Farrow, the manager of Avenue Taxis in Ipswich, said: 'I have had our regular customers ringing up and wanting assurances about our drivers. I can say that they are police checked, but all that means is that they haven't been caught for anything.' Taxi companies had taken to sending text messages to customers giving the registration number and a physical description of the driver coming to pick them up, so widespread was the concern for safety. One young woman told the media: 'My birthday's on Monday. I was going to celebrate in town. Now I'm staying in.'

The reaction among prostitutes working in Ipswich was no different. But whilst their numbers had sharply decreased on the streets, amazingly there was still a hardcore continuing to work. Lou, the twenty-eight-year-old prostitute who was interviewed numerous times by the media during those days, was still there.

In an interview with the *Mirror*, Lou said: 'I have no choice because I need the cash. If I wasn't working here I would be shoplifting; then I would land up in prison. Of course I'm scared. It's a difficult situation. You have to try and make a snap judgement about men before you get in a car with them.'

Just like the rest of the Ipswich population, the prostitutes themselves had their theories about the identity of the killer. These were generally based on a client looking or behaving strangely or not coming to look for a girl any more. However, because of the now huge police presence this is perhaps understandable. Lou continued: 'This guy needs to be caught by the police quickly before he strikes again. You can't help worrying who might be next.'

Another woman working as a prostitute, Katie, aged twenty-three, said: 'Of course it has made me worried, but I have got a heroin habit and I need the money to pay my rent. It's dangerous out on the streets. You just have to do your best to look after yourself. When a man stops for me, I am in his face asking who he is and what he's doing.'

The impact of the Ipswich murders was now also being felt far outside the town due to the media coverage. Of course this cannot be compared with the effect on the families of the victims, or to a much lesser extent the general Ipswich population, but there was a significant ripple. Every evening and night the main news bulletins were now leading with the story and the national newspapers led with it on their front pages most days. Suddenly the poisoning of an ex-KGB agent in London, which had been a huge story over the previous weeks, was being supplanted.

The Ipswich murders were now ingrained in the British public consciousness. People all over Britain were waiting for the next development, hoping for an arrest. The wider world was now also becoming aware of the tragic sequence of events. One only has to look at the online condolence books set up by the Ipswich *Evening Star* for the victims to read emails sent from literally all over the world.

On the evening of 13 December the British Comedy Awards were held in London and the American film director Oliver Stone made an appearance there. When he addressed the audience he reportedly said: 'I haven't been here for years. Jack the Ripper's back – it's good to see nothing changes.' The audience reacted with stunned silence.

At the beginning it had seemed like the isolated murder of a prostitute in a small English town. This had developed into the murders of five young women working as prostitutes. With Christmas now less than two weeks away, the vibrations of this macabre phenomenon were reaching out beyond Ipswich, across Britain, and now on an international stage. Public awareness was now very wide, but the public could only hope that the police were becoming more focused in their massive murder hunt and getting closer to the Ipswich serial killer. The police knew that they had to try to understand the psychology behind these extreme actions, and use this understanding to close in.

The views of several leading criminal and forensic psychologists were printed in the newspapers at this time, as well as experts appearing on the television news as talking heads. Whilst there was inevitably much speculation, some of the scientific approaches were informative.

The key areas that needed to be investigated on a fundamental level were access, opportunity and motive, according to Professor David Wilson from the Department of Criminology at the University of Central England in a profile produced for the *Sun* newspaper. An examination of his theories is useful here.

First, there is the area of access. Prostitutes are the easiest targets for any killer as they put themselves in vulnerable situations in secluded places. As all five of the Ipswich victims had worked in the town's red light district, this would have given the killer easy access, and in the view of Professor Wilson, the killer would have been in control of the situation.

With regard to opportunity, Professor Wilson asserted that the killer might have wanted to kill for a long time but without having had the opportunity. This could have been because he had been in prison or because he felt that the risks and consequences were too great; factors such as CCTV and other security methods might have prevented any further fantasies becoming reality. Finally, the killer might have been in a rewarding relationship previously, but this might now have come to an end. Above all Professor David Wilson emphasised that taking advantage of any opportunity to kill takes creative thinking and planning.

Coming to motive, Professor Wilson looks at four areas: how the victims were chosen, how they were treated, the forensic evidence gathered, and the method of disposal of the bodies. He was an 'organised' killer in Professor Wilson's opinion and he cited three points to back up his case. First, the killer appeared to be careful about leaving forensic clues by removing the clothing of the women and leaving the first two in water. Second, the killer seemed to know the roads well around Ipswich and may have planned the routes he would use. Third, the killer would have had to appear as relatively ordinary to the women to be accepted as a client, as a 'disorganised' individual might have aroused their suspicions.

The four main types of serial killer should also be looked into here. There is the *visionary killer*, who hears voices from God or the Devil and is instructed by this other-worldly force to kill 'unclean' prostitutes. Then there is the *mission killer*, who feels the compulsion to clean up the streets. Next there is the *hedonistic killer*, who has no higher motive than to gain thrills, no matter what the consequences are. Finally, the *power/control killer* needs to feel power and a sense of mastery over his helpless victims. As discussed earlier, the latter is perhaps particularly pertinent to the case of the Ipswich killer.

Professor David Wilson thought overall that the Ipswich killer was a visionary killer and that he had wanted to kill for some time. He went on to issue a warning: 'The time between the murders is becoming shorter, and this might indicate a frenzy – he must be caught quickly.'

Meanwhile, Dr Keith Ashcroft, a consultant forensic psychologist who was trained by the FBI, took the view that the Ipswich killer was taunting the police. He felt that the killer showed a large awareness of the media spotlight on the crimes and that this was feeding an ego or egos. He added that it was very possible that another person was involved as an assistant or accomplice. Professor David Canter, the leading geographical and psychological criminal profiler from the University of Liverpool, agreed with this theory about an evil double act.

With regard to the killer being publicity hungry, this does appear plausible. The bodies had been left in increasingly open spaces, with little attempt at concealment, almost as if the killer wanted them to be found quickly and therefore fuel the infamy surrounding the crimes. Or was this growing disregard the result of a frenzy, with the killer simply becoming more careless, as suggested by Professor David Wilson?

The leading writer and criminologist Colin Wilson said that the killer could be a woman-hater. This form of extreme misogyny has been observed in other serial killers, often in relation to the mother of the killer or his relationships with women in general. But essentially this is still largely a power issue. Mr Wilson also observed that it seemed like 'the end of a cycle, not the start'. This might explain why the speed was increasing and the fear of detection was receding in the mind of the killer. Perhaps he was now past caring and the compulsion he felt simply could not be controlled.

Dr Joseph Diaz, an Associate Professor of Criminology at Fayetteville State University in North Carolina, USA, stated that the killer 'could be a strongly built virgin in his late twenties or early thirties from the Ipswich area with a sexual problem'.

Mike Berry, a criminal psychologist at Manchester Metropolitan University, said that in his opinion the killer could be a local Ipswich man such as a taxi driver or a nurse, or even a policeman, and aged between twenty-five and forty.

In a conversation with this author, Dr Glenn Wilson, a specialist psychologist in deviant sexual behaviour at King's College, London, confirmed the profile that he had given to the *Sun*: 'It is normal for a serial killer to go to ground or move their area of attack after so much attention is focused on them. But it's possible the exact opposite is happening here. He seems to be racing against time to kill as many times as possible before he is caught. And he is certainly not going to stop until he is caught. He is killing at a much faster rate than Peter Sutcliffe [the Yorkshire Ripper] did, possibly because he fears he could get caught at any moment and wants to pack in as much excitement as possible. He is not cooling off. His campaign is heating up.'

This certainly supports the idea that the killer had reached some level of frenzy, a form of rampage, or as Dr Glenn Wilson described it, 'a kind of pre-Christmas spree'. If this was the case, then it was obviously even more imperative that the offender should be caught quickly. Dr Wilson went on:

'It's interesting there is no sign of mutilation of the bodies and that they are found naked. This suggests that he might kill them and simply want to spend time with them. Being with them when they are dead may be the only way he can feel comfortable with women.'

This idea that the killer wanted the victims to be pliable in his hands and not able to answer back is a very significant one. Just being with them might have been enough, but other activities may have taken place, such as obscene posing, masturbation and talking to the women; either one or all could have been performed post-mortem. This brings us back to the concept of power and control, something that the killer perhaps did not feel he had in his normal relationships with women.

In conversation with this author, Dr Glenn Wilson also asserted that the killer was likely to have a 'transient work history' and an unstable lifestyle. But this latter point does not mean that the killer would be disorganised in his approach to the murders. It is quite possible for somebody with an unsettled life to be an organised killer – after all, this is the one area of his life he may feel he has control over.

The clinical way that the Ipswich victims were left, often close together, in the words of a detective on the case showed 'a chilling arrogance and indifference'. The same source said: 'This monster treats these girls' bodies like bags of rubbish and just dumps them in isolated spots.'

So how much control did the killer have over what they were doing? Was it a pure form of frenzy spiralling more and more out of control? Or was the killer capable of rationally enjoying the resultant massive publicity and the thrill of the manhunt? The police were in little doubt that the latter was the case. A police source said on 12 December, after the bodies of Paula Clennell and Annette Nicholls were discovered: 'Whoever is behind this is clearly getting his kicks not only from what they are doing, but also the publicity surrounding the killings.'

By dumping more and more bodies around Ipswich, the killer was exerting a form of control over the police, playing a sick cat and mouse game, where he or they held the rules. The police had no idea where a victim would be taken from next (although the likeliest place was the red light area), or where and when she would be found. Did the killer or killers get off on this, smiling when the blanket coverage appeared on the television screen or in the newspapers?

So much would rest on the forensic evidence of course, and the fact that the last three bodies to be found were not in water meant that there was a greater chance of clues being discovered. But if the experts were right, then it was truly frightening. If it was approaching frenzy, then anything could happen. It might seem more reassuring if the murders were at the end of a cycle (remembering that unsolved murders from years earlier were being looked into), but that is not necessarily true. It might mean that the killer would want to go out with a bang and the climax could mean further tragedies.

The importance of fantasy and the dangerous spilling over of violent fantasies into the reality of a serial killer were explored earlier. But what are the factors that provide a breeding ground for these fantasies and for the development of the abnormal psychology that in extremely rare cases leads to serial murder? The seeds are sown in childhood and adolescence.

In their book *Abnormal Child and Adolescent Psychology*, published in 2003, Jean E. Dumas and Wendy J. Nilsen explain: 'Children and adolescents are exposed to very important psychological influences from family and peers.' This might sound obvious, but it cannot be emphasised enough in of the case of a serial killer like the Ipswich offender. What occurs in the early years may help to explain the extreme actions of later life.

Dumas and Nilsen go on to say:

'Youth who grow up in families where they receive inadequate care or where adults struggle with depression, alcoholism or other problems are at increased risk of developing one or more psychological disorders. The same is true of youth who are isolated or rejected by peers at school or in the community.'

This lack of affection and attention from parents or the feelings of isolation that can build up when a child's peers reject or ostracise him can only feed such a child's private fantasy world. And if the rejection and feelings of isolation or not belonging are prolonged enough, this could lead to violent fantasies in cases where a child has a predisposition in that direction.

There are six areas that can help to detect the development of abnormal psychology. First, there is attachment, referring to the strength of the bond between the child and the parent or carer. If there is a lack of affection or care given, especially over a long period of time, this can be very damaging.

Second, parenting is crucial in the development of a child's healthy psychology. This dictates the level of attachment the child feels to parents or the closest carer. The attitudes, skills and beliefs that the parent or carer brings to the task of bringing up the child are basic factors in the child's psychological development.

Then there is the stress of relationships. If family relationships are especially stressful, these can taint and warp the child's psychological development and in some cases lead to disorders.

Next, the influence of peers is very important. Peer pressure can work both ways, exerting both positive and negative effects, and a healthy child develops a way of coping with this. Good relationships with peers can sometimes offset some of the negative effects of poor parental relationships. On the other hand, as we have seen earlier, peers can introduce a young person to damaging or risky behaviours, such as drug-taking.

Then there are sociological and cultural influences. The neighbourhood in which the child is brought up, the beliefs and expectations of those around, for themselves and for him, and the status of his family and himself in that environment. All of these are vital to healthy psychological development.

Finally, there are historical influences and trends in society. Since the Second World War, families in Britain have generally become more dysfunctional and there has been a breakdown in community life. This has had an impact on the way that a child develops, perceives himself and reacts to the world.

These are of course general factors, but if applied to somebody with an abnormal psychology, they can help to explain how the fantasy life of a serial killer such as the Ipswich killer was allowed to develop. This process takes years and the killer may have shown few or no obvious signs of abnormality. By 2006 the Ipswich killer's abnormal psychology had fully crystallised and the fantasy had already become reality, bringing tragic consequences. It was highly probable that there would be a history of pointers to his abnormality if and when he was caught.

The shock of the double discovery of 12 December was now just beginning to sink in. With five victims so far the pressure was intensifying. The police were working all out for a result, working against a clock that must have seemed to tick inside their own heads. On that day 2,199 telephone calls were taken from the public at the police incident room. DCS Gull reiterated the fact that the manhunt was the largest ever seen in the area, that more than thirty officers had already joined the inquiry from other police forces and that more were expected.

By 14 December the number of calls to the police incident room had reached 5,500, along with 1,000 emails. On the same day it was confirmed that Paula Clennell had died as a result of 'compression to the neck'. The Home Office pathologist Nat Carey carried out the post-mortems on both Paula Clennell and Annette Nicholls. On 15 December, it was announced that no definitive cause of death had been found in the case of Annette Nicholls.

A candlelit service was held at St Peter's Church, Copdock, close to where Paula and Annette were found. It was hoped that it would be of comfort to their families and friends.

On 16 December a minute's silence was held at Ipswich Town's Portman Road football ground before the start of their match against Leeds United. The ground is just a few minutes from where the women had worked.

On 17 December the police were talking to passengers at the railway stations along the line used by Anneli Alderton a week before her body was discovered. On the same day, the Home Office Minister Fiona MacTaggart was encouraging other ministers to implement a plan to legalise small brothels.

Thankfully over the previous five days no more bodies had been found. Another prostitute who had been reported missing was located alive and well, to much relief. But the police knew that it was probably only a matter of time before they were called out to another terrible scene. The waiting must have been the worst part, but the Suffolk Police were too busy to let this become an issue. The five separate murder inquiries were now formed into one huge manhunt and key suspects were being zeroed in on.

The need for a strong lead was immense, the desire for enough evidence to make an arrest desperate. The tension in the air was palpable. The world media was watching and the people of Ipswich blinked in the unprecedented spotlight on their town, while the families of five women suffered immeasurably in their midst. The police were feeling the heat the most, their professional sense of duty intensified by what was now becoming a personal crusade for many officers. The leads were mounting and the jigsaw was slowly forming a recognisable picture. But would they complete enough of it before another young woman was killed?

CHAPTER FIVE

A NERVY DEVELOPMENT

MONDAY, 18 DECEMBER 2006
TRIMLEY ST MARTIN, SUFFOLK
7.20am

The village of Trimley St Martin is located to the east of Ipswich, and close to the A14 road between Ipswich and Felixstowe. It is much closer to the port town of Felixstowe than Ipswich and locally the village is known simply as Trimley. It was there that the police focused on a specific site. That site was a very ordinary semi-detached house worth just under a hundred thousand pounds in a quiet cul-de-sac, the kind of place where curtains twitch regularly. And this time the focus of police activity was not dead but very much alive. As those in houses around were giving their newly holidaying children breakfast, and while people across the country were getting ready for those final days of work before the festive break, the police swooped.

The effect of such a sudden intrusion to the early

morning peace was stark. As in all serious crime and terrorist arrests, it was essential for the police to have the element of surprise at the moment of capture. However, the target that morning had more than some inkling that it might happen. Likewise, although the local Trimley community was in shock that day and in the coming days, they had already witnessed some discreet police activity centred on the house in Jubilee Close in the previous weeks.

The man they took away was called Tom Stephens and he was thirty-seven years old. Mr Stephens worked at the Tesco supermarket in nearby Martlesham, where his job title was 'team leader'. He had also worked part-time as a taxi driver. He lived in the house alone.

Stephens was taken to an unnamed police station in Suffolk, this secrecy being necessary because of the media circus that would have converged on that location. Also, the police were taking no chances with the local feelings of anger and hatred directed at the Ipswich killer. While Stephens was held in custody on the suspicion of murdering Gemma, Tania, Anneli, Paula and Annette, a police team was searching his mother's house in the quaint market town of Eye, Suffolk, where Stephens had lived at one time.

Tom Stephens had lived in the house in Jubilee Close for only about three months. He had in fact been questioned by the police four times before his arrest, once in a car and three times at Ipswich police stations. The first occasion had been soon after Tania Nicol disappeared on 30 October. He sat with two officers in a police car for an hour and answered their questions. He was then taken to a police station and interviewed again on tape to ensure nothing he said could be lost. This interview was conducted under caution.

The police also searched his house on 22 November as part of ongoing enquiries. They were in the house for several hours in the morning and two groups of police officers were involved. The first were forensic officers in plastic suits and then the plain-clothed second group went into the house after it had been searched. Afterwards, his car was searched and Stephens was later to complain that they had flattened his car battery.

So when the police entered No. 8 Jubilee Close that chilly December morning there had been a build-up of the investigation into Stephens as a suspect. His garden had even been scanned by a metal detector almost a month before his arrest. But in the end, much of the suspicion that fell on Stephens was actually fuelled by words from his own mouth.

Detective Chief Superintendent Stewart Gull said that day concerning Stephens: 'We will not be naming the police station where the man is being held. As legal proceedings are now active, Suffolk Police will not be issuing further comments or appeals at this stage.'

The legal terms of the arrest of Stephens were as follows – he could be held for twenty-four hours from the moment he was booked into custody at the police station, and then a further twelve hours could be given with the authorisation of a police superintendent, and up to a further ninety-six hours with the permission of the court. At the end of this time he would either have to be charged or released.

Within an hour the news was all over the internet and on the television news. The twenty-four-hour news channels paid close attention to the events going on in Trimley, and the police tape around 8 Jubilee Close with officers guarding outside was broadcast for long periods of time, interviews with on-the-spot (or newly arrived) correspondents going out on air. Talking heads and interviews with locals were hitting the screens and within a few hours interviews with people who knew Stephens were on the evening news and in the evening papers. It was very big news, the first arrest of the whole inquiry.

The last time that the area around Trimley had been in the headlines was in 1999, seven years earlier, when the body of seventeen-year-old Vicky Hall was found in a water-filled ditch about 25 miles (40km) away. She had been in a nightclub in Felixstowe the last time she was seen. Although it was not definitive, it was possible that Vicky Hall had been asphyxiated. But the police had not formally linked this case with the murders of the five Ipswich women and they were not able to confirm to the media if Stephens would be questioned about Vicky Hall's murder. This murder had in fact occurred years before Stephens had moved to Trimley.

The police did not name Tom Stephens to the media. Any suspect is allowed anonymity until formally charged; nevertheless the media had named him and run photographs of him before the end of the day. This was a fairly unusual action and will be discussed later. If Stephens was innocent, then his reputation would be unfairly in tatters, but then Stephens himself had been very forthcoming with the media before his arrest.

A sense of some relief was already pulsing through Ipswich and the media were all too ready to paint Stephens in a sinister light. The police were much more cautious, telling prostitutes to continue to stay away from the streets. However, some of the facts spoke for themselves. He had known all five victims. He reportedly used prostitutes. Allegedly, he had called a prostitute the night before his arrest, 'begging' for sex. But was he the killer?

One of the major sources of information available to the media and therefore the public about Tom Stephens in the days after his arrest did not come from those who lived around him in Trimley or from family, friends and colleagues. It came from Stephens himself.

The emergence of the internet and cyberspace has revolutionised the way that we communicate and get our information. The first years of the twenty-first century have seen the appearance of various social networking websites where people can make new friends or reacquaint themselves with old ones. These are sites such as MySpace, Facebook and Friends Reunited. Tom Stephens last logged on to his MySpace page on 27 October 2006, just three days before the disappearance of the first of the Ipswich victims. Tania Nicol was last seen on 30 October and, coupled with the fact that Stephens had been closest to Tania out of all of the five women, this soon led to many rumours and speculations about why he had not logged on to MySpace since 27 October.

It must be said that at first glance the MySpace page created by Stephens did not show him in a sympathetic light in the context of following events. But of course it has to be remembered that when people set up such internet portals, they often exaggerate and distort their true selves, presenting a wacky image in order to shock mildly and catch the eye of internet surfers.

Many people who create a MySpace page choose a nickname to head their profile. Tom Stephens called himself 'the Bishop' after a character in the recent superhero film X-Men. But this name was a godsend to the media, which used it again and again over the coming days in reports about Stephens. This went some way to branding him in the public consciousness – a grown man who named himself after a superhero.

The main photograph of Stephens on his profile pictured him wearing a floppy fishing hat and grinning inanely, in medium close-up and looking directly into the camera. Another smaller photo showed him wearing a Union Jack tie. In yet another he was seen looking mildly amused and clutching a tin of Bird's custard powder. A further image had him in a garden clearing sitting in some sort of cart, and another is a view of his face from a lower angle. This latter was precisely the kind of picture you get when you hold a digital camera in front of you and take a photograph of yourself.

The most arresting image of Stephens on his profile was one where he was again pictured close up, but straight on this time. He had his eyes closed, but he had (or somebody else had) drawn pupils on both of his eyelids, giving the impression that those were his real eyes. At first sight this photo is eye-catching and faintly sinister. However, all in all, the photographs of Stephens on MySpace show somebody desperate to appear interesting, employing mild shock tactics to do so.

In the 'here for' section of his profile, where users are invited to explain why they are on MySpace, Stephens' entry read: 'Dating, serious relationships, friends'. In the place where he was asked whether he had any children or would like any in the future, Stephens had entered that he 'loves kids, but not for me'. He described himself as 'straight' and single and said that he was athletic. He listed his hobbies as 'most types of keeping fit' and going on days and nights out. When asked to talk about his favourite film, he said 'Sorry I haven't starred in any', and said that he did not watch television much.

In the area reserved for job or company, Stephens stated that he worked for Tesco as a team leader, and had done 'from 1997 until they sack me'. Under the education section, he said that he was educated to 'high school' level, and that he had gone to Thorpe St Andrews School between 1980 and 1987, a specialist sports college.

There were also some images of 'Hong Kong Phooey', on his page; Stephens said that the cartoon character from the 1970s was 'my hero'.

When all of these elements are added together, and topped by the fact that his MySpace page had a piece of classical music, Canon in D major by Johann Pachelbel, playing in the background when his profile was opened, one can get a sense of the flavour of the webpage. It is gently surreal, in the tradition of British humour such as 'The Goons' and 'Monty Python'. It is not a disturbing portrait that comes together here. What emerges is a profile created by a somewhat lonely man approaching middle age, who wants to meet a partner and friends. To attract attention he emphasised the zany side of his character and a quick trawl through MySpace pages shows this to be far from out of the ordinary.

Within twenty-four hours of Tom Stephens being arrested, MySpace deleted his account, but the media had already got all the information it needed. The MySpace profile would give the media the fuel to depict Stephens as something of a misfit or loner and with many hoping that the police had found the Ipswich killer, Stephens seemed to fit the bill. In reality, he was like so many others. But nobody knew if he was a serial killer or involved in some way, so final judgement had to be reserved.

Just before his MySpace profile was removed, Tom Stephens had eight 'friends' listed. But there was only one message left: 'Heya Tom crazy football guy, greets from Germany.'

Tom Stephens was born in Ipswich in May 1969 but did not grow up there. When he was still very young his parents Ellen and Douglas divorced, and Tom and his younger brother Jack moved with their mother to Blowfield, near Norwich, where Ellen became a primary school teacher. Between 1980 and 1987, Tom did indeed go to Thorpe St Andrews School in Norwich, a specialist sports college.

Stephens was always athletic and was remembered by contemporaries at school as a quiet boy. One schoolfriend remembered him: 'He used to wear really tight trousers, he was very uncool. He would hang around on the outside of groups, a bit of a nerd.' Stephens loved sport and had a passion for football, but this was not the angle focused on by the media.

At the age of twenty-three in 1992, Stephens was living and working in Norwich as a special constable with the Norfolk Police. He enjoyed this job, which involved patrolling the centre of Norwich and inevitably included Norwich's red light district. The fact that he was at one time employed by the police, even in a subsidiary role, was much focused on by the newspapers, providing a controversial angle – the ex-special police constable being questioned by the police was somewhat ironic.

Tom Stephens remained a special constable for five years until 1997, then leaving Norwich and returning to Ipswich where he was born. In February 1998 he got married to a local nurse, Judith Kirk, and they lived in a semi-detached house in Cavendish Street, on the eastern edges of Ipswich town centre, not far from Suffolk College, where both Gemma Adams and Annette Nicholls had studied. Stephens worked at the Tesco supermarket in the village of Martlesham, east of Ipswich.

The marriage lasted for five years, but in 2003 they separated and this would lead to a reportedly bitter divorce. Stephens was now about thirty-four and he moved into a flat, sharing with three others in Pearson Road, further away from the town centre to the east. He continued working at Tesco in Martlesham, which had become a twenty-four-hour store, and worked shifts there, cycling 5 miles (8km) to get there.

Stuart Kantor, the estate manager who controlled the flat in Pearson Road, and so was effectively Stephens' landlord, told the *Guardian*: 'He was an ordinary tenant. He never held parties, he was never noisy. We are all amazed that anyone like that could be arrested.'

Stephens was rumoured to have inherited some money and in September 2006 he moved to No. 8 Jubilee Close, Trimley St Martin, near Felixstowe. By now he had a car, a purple Renault Clio, which he used to get to work and, as he said himself, to ferry around some of the women working as prostitutes in Ipswich. The car was towed away on a flatbed lorry on the morning he was arrested.

His close neighbours said that they did not know Stephens well. He was said not even to acknowledge them when he took out his rubbish to be collected, and one neighbour told the *Sun* that he walked around in tiny shorts, regardless of the temperature outside.

It seems that Tom Stephens began making trips to Ipswich's red light district around eighteen months before he was arrested, so some time in mid-2004. He admitted that he regularly paid for sex and that he ran errands for the working girls, often driving them around as well. It was alleged in the *Sun* that Stephens sometimes asked for sexual favours from the girls in return for driving them home. One Ipswich prostitute, Katie, told that newspaper: 'The dead girls were my friends. We thought of Tom as quite a sad, lonely bloke. He used to say "Girls don't like me" and "What would a girl like you want with me?" I think he liked working girls because he could get closer to them than other women.'

The picture that emerged of Stephens was that he was often hanging around the women in the red light district, having chats and seeing if they needed anything. He seems to have been seen as an errand boy. Katie said: 'Tom was there for us on tap.' He liked to think that he was looking out for them and that they were his true friends. But none of the women who knew Tom Stephens were remotely frightened of him or thought he could have killed anyone. Jacci Goldsmith, an ex-prostitute who was also a friend of Stephens, told the *Sun*: 'He was nice and sweet, with no nasty bone in his body. He has not got it in him to hurt anyone. I can't believe he has done any wrong.'

Stephens had many of the telephone numbers of the

Ipswich prostitutes and since the tragedies had started happening he often called them to make sure they were safe. As Jacci Goldsmith told the *Guardian*: 'He just wanted to chat because he was upset and pretty down... Most of the girls who were working would have known Tom. The girls trusted him.'

However, Jacci Goldsmith went on: 'For the girls he was just another punter. He was a bit persistent. He would hang about...outside their houses.' But one aspect of Stephens' arrest was especially confusing to Jacci Goldsmith. It was the fact that none of the victims showed any sign of sexual assault. In her words, Stephens was preoccupied with sex: 'He's after sex. He's all for sex.'

It was obvious that Stephens had a shadowy life, spending much of his free time with prostitutes, paying for sex, driving them around and doing other favours for them, sometimes in return for sexual services. The image of Stephens here is certainly of a very lonely man, willing to pay for what he regarded as friendship and feeling valued as a 'protector' of the vulnerable women, many of whom were also drug addicts. It is possible that he felt like an outsider in society himself to some degree and so related to and empathised with these women.

It was becoming clear that although Stephens had known all five women who became victims of the Ipswich killer, he knew Tania Nicol and Gemma Adams the best. The closest relationship he had was probably with nineteen-year-old Tania and it was reported that it was Stephens who had bought Tania the shiny stiletto shoes she was wearing the night she disappeared and which the police were still frantically looking for – another client had previously been thought to have bought them. But

Stephens also said that he was the closest thing that Annette Nicholls had as a boyfriend, too.

When the media tried to contact Stephens' ex-wife Judith, she was unavailable for comment. A close friend said that Judith was 'very upset...she asked me not to say anything if anyone came round here.'

Tom Stephens' father was tracked down by the *Guardian*, and from his home in Northamptonshire Douglas Stephens said: 'There is nothing I can say. I am his father yes, but I don't want to say anything further.'

Tom's mother Ellen was likewise found at her home in Eye, Suffolk, where the police had been searching. Her new husband just said that Ellen was unwell. Stephens had visited her regularly during her illness and he said himself that news of his involvement with prostitutes and his friendship with the five murdered women had come as a big shock to her.

An unnamed close friend of Tom Stephens told the *Sun* that Stephens was intelligent and 'he loves literature, sports and eighteenth-century Suffolk history'. The friend also added that Stephens was 'very lonely' and that his life had fallen apart when his marriage broke up.

All of these glimpses into the life of Tom Stephens paint a picture of him, but perhaps what can give us the greatest insight are the words that came from Stephens himself.

On Sunday, 17 December, the day before he was arrested, the *Sunday Mirror* ran a long interview with Tom Stephens. Stephens had allegedly spoken to the media for a fee. During the course of the interview, Stephens broke down in sobs several times. Many revelations would come from the interview, including Stephens admitting that he did not have any alibis for the times when the five Ipswich women disappeared. He also said that he could get arrested. The attentions of the police over the previous weeks had obviously got to him. However, some of the phrasing he uses is either suspicious or unfortunate.

It is probably true that this interview helped the police to make up their minds to arrest him. The interview was conducted in a pub car park close to Stephens' home in Trimley by the *Sunday Mirror* reporter Michael Duffy. It is worth quoting at length here.

Stephens emphasised how well he knew the five women:

'Gemma and Tania, the ones I was closest to, are the best-looking girls who do this in Ipswich. In fact, they were probably the top five. Over time I have been involved with most of the girls. If you count, there are about fifty over the last year.'

When asked if he was worried about being 'in the frame' for the murders, having already been questioned four times and his house and car searched, Stephens said:

'I could get arrested. That is quite likely, let's not say likely, let's say possible. If a car very like mine is seen in the area – up a lane somewhere – then I'd expect police would arrest me and question me very hard... I would have [had] complete opportunity, the girls would have trusted me so much. If I had blindfolded them and taken them to the edge of a cliff and said take two steps but take three steps and you'll go over – they would have taken the two steps. From the police profiling it does look like me – white male between twenty-five and forty, knows the area, works strange hours. The bodies have got close to my house [Levington, where Paula and Annette were found on 12 December is just over 2 miles (3.2km) away]. I know that I'm innocent. But I don't have alibis for some of the times – actually I'm not entirely sure I have tight alibis for any of the times.'

When the interviewer said that he thought Stephens had been ruled out by the police, but that now (after Stephens' comments) he would be taking a closer look at Stephens if it were his job to catch the killer, Stephens said:

'Don't think I'm pointing out my guilt, because this is almost the worst example to give, but in the case of the Yorkshire Ripper he was arrested, released and later charged [untrue – Sutcliffe had been questioned before his final arrest, but never previously arrested for the Ripper murders]. But in his case he was obviously guilty, but at that point they thought he was innocent.'

The interviewer then asked Stephens about Tania Nicol:

'She was a lovely, sweet girl. It's so easy to believe her mother didn't know what she was doing because she didn't fit the image at all...she would sometimes stay overnight with a client – it was better money. She would always tell her mother she was just staying at a friend's place. She was nineteen, a little bit crazy, but no crazier than half a million nineteen-year-olds across the country.'

When asked if he had loved Tania, Stephens replied:

'No. But Annette thought we were together. We weren't boyfriend and girlfriend, but I was the closest thing she had to a boyfriend and in behaviour she was the closest thing I had to a girlfriend. I didn't love her. But I should have been there for her.'

In the interview, Stephens would go on to say how guilty he felt at not having been able to protect the women. When asked why, as it had not been Stephens' job to protect them, Stephens said that that was the relationship he had had with the women. When the interviewer asked if this made Stephens feel needed, Stephens broke down in tears.

The interviewer pressed Stephens on how he had first got involved with the girls, Stephens asked him to guess. The interviewer said that he guessed Stephens had 'started out as a punter and grew close to the girls' and Stephens said that 'if you're not at the centre of the dartboard, then you're darn close'. Stephens then burst into tears again.

When asked why he spent time with drug-addicted prostitutes when he was intelligent and good-looking, Stephens said: 'On paper I should be attractive, but there's something about me women do not like.'

Asked how his family felt about his involvement in the world of prostitution, Stephens said that he had only told his mother that day [17 December] and that it had come as a 'bolt from the blue' to her. He described himself as 'a terrible son, she is very ill. I was supposed to be looking after her on Monday [the next day, when he was arrested] but I don't know whether I'm up to it now.'

The interviewer wondered how Stephens could find common ground with the prostitutes and Stephens said:

'I'm sad and lonely. I made compromises on my morals to go down [to the red light district] the first time, so I suppose getting involved with them isn't a huge leap. If you want to have any relationship with a working girl you have to accept the drugs. They work to do drugs as much as they breathe to live.'

Stephens was asked if he knew who the pimps were in Ipswich and he said:

'There are no pimps in Ipswich. I know nothing about massage parlours, but there are no pimps who run a number of girls [on the streets]. I suppose my actions – by the legal definition I'm nowhere near that. But by my behaviour, I'd be as close as there was to a pimp. I knew a lot of girls and I used to run them about. If there was such a thing as a pimp he'd take money for it.'

When pushed to say whether he ever took money, Stephens said:

'I used to occasionally take petrol money, but I certainly wouldn't have filled up on what I was getting. Some of the girls have boyfriends who are dominant over them, forcing them to work and supporting their habit as well. That's about as close as there is to a pimp in Ipswich. There is so much lying that goes on with the girls you have to be very careful.'

Finally Stephens states his position:

> 'I know I am innocent and I am certain it won't go as far as me being charged. I am completely confident of that. It's not unusual for someone to be arrested, released without charge and then someone else be arrested and charged.'

Above all Tom Stephens shows himself to be very self-aware and he clearly understands the position he is in. There are some hints that he is enjoying being the centre of attention, especially when he is talking about his relationships with the working girls. And it must be remembered that Stephens chose to give this lengthy interview; he was under no obligation to do so. If there was a fee involved, it may have been an incentive. He may also have thought that this was an opportunity to put his side of the story across.

People in his community were no doubt already whispering about him before his arrest, as the police had already searched his house.

Stephens described himself as 'sad and lonely' and this impression comes across strongly. He seems very vulnerable, has low self-esteem and is very insecure about the effect he has on women. The prostitutes he befriended, including the five women tragically murdered, especially Tania, Gemma and Annette, do seem to have been the focus of his social life. Perhaps the vulnerable can understand the vulnerable. But were his seemingly candid statements masking a deeper guilt? That is what the police had to find out.

On the same day that Tom Stephens was arrested, 18 December, another interview that he had given was released. In the previous week he had given an interview to the BBC reporter Trudi Barber. Stephens had agreed to the interview on the understanding that it was only going to be used for background purposes only and that it would not be broadcast. The BBC had made the interview available to the police.

But there would be some criticism aimed at the BBC for releasing the details of this interview to the wider media after an agreement had been made with Stephens. It was of course necessary for it to be made available to the police, but the rest of the media had no such need to know its content. Along with the naming of Stephens before he was charged, this would add to the negative view of the media handling of the case in some quarters.

In this interview Stephens said that he had known Gemma Adams for eighteen months and Tania Nicol for six. He emphasised that his relationship with Tania was the closest. He said that he knew Annette Nicholls, but this time he had described himself as 'the closest thing Tania had as a boyfriend' and that 'neither of us were faithful to the other one'. In the *Sunday Mirror* interview, given a few days later, Stephens had said that he was 'the closest thing Annette had to a boyfriend'. However, he had made it clear that he and Annette were not boyfriend and girlfriend.

He also said: 'I didn't know Anneli at all. I've only ever spoken to her since both Gemma and Tania went missing, partly to say, if you know anything, please talk to the police and if you won't talk to the police, please talk to me and I'll talk to the police.'

He added that he had also wanted to check if she was all right (before she disappeared) and that he had spoken to other girls whom he did not know in the same way.

Stephens explained how he got to know the woman:

'I wanted to chat with the girl, before and after [sex], which is partly why I was always happy to give them a lift... They'd quite often want a lift to get their drugs and I would give them a lift, and it was better for me like that and that's how it developed into a friendship with a number of the girls.'

The police were very cautious regarding what they said about Tom Stephens. It was known that he had been arrested and was being held for questioning in custody, but he had not been charged yet with any offence. They said that Stephens' arrest was 'of interest' but no stronger than that. A police source said: 'Investigations are continuing, looking at a number of other suspects.'

In an interview with BBC News, Roy Ramm, a former Scotland Yard Commander, said:

'In any investigation like this, when you've got a number of young women who are all doing the same kind of thing, they're all acting as prostitutes in a very small area, it's not inconceivable that a number of people will know all these young women, and could know them innocently. So I think the police will be proceeding very cautiously here.'

The scale of the Ipswich murder inquiry was now such that there were now several very strong suspects and many more peripheral ones. Tom Stephens was obviously just one strong suspect, but he may have been arrested only so that the police could get more information from him under controlled conditions and for an extended period of time. At the end of that time they would either charge him or release him, depending on how satisfied they were with his answers.

The Association of Chief Police Officers said on 18 December that the police National Information and Co-ordination Centre had arranged for the biggest deployment of forces outside Suffolk to help in a murder inquiry. Thirty-six police forces had sent 412 detectives, uniformed officers and police staff to help with the hunt, a truly staggering number, and a reflection of the seriousness with which the Ipswich murders were regarded. This was in addition to 160 Suffolk police officers working on the inquiry by that time.

The clothes worn by Gemma, Tania, Anneli, Paula and Annette were a continuing focus for the police. They believed the clothes could give up DNA evidence and unlock the identity of the serial killer or killers. There was still no certainty over whether the murders had been committed by one or more persons and the police had to keep an open mind on this.

The bodies were all being examined by toxicologists in the laboratory too, as it was thought that the victims might have been drugged or gassed in order to incapacitate them, largely because of the absence of defence wounds. The police confirmed that they were no longer looking for a murder weapon in relation to the murders.

The police were continuing to interview clients of the women, but DCS Gull said that 'Nobody has been spoken to as a suspect at this time.' This reveals that Tom Stephens had not been such a strong lead as a suspect after all. It does make one wonder if his own words to the media had led directly to his arrest the following day, as his house and car had already been searched and items taken away, and he had been questioned four times without having being arrested.

The police had also contacted Interpol as it was speculated that the killer might have already left Britain. The fact that no bodies had been found for almost a week supported this, but in reality nobody really knew if a body would be found the next day. One theory was that the killer could have left Britain through the port of Felixstowe and could by then have been on the European mainland.

By 18 December the police had taken 9,000 phone calls from the public and looked through about 10,000 hours of CCTV footage. They were also still going through the list of 400 known Suffolk sex offenders and checking through blacklists of violent clients kept by local prostitutes and massage parlours. Any one of these avenues might have produced a break and led to the killer.

Tom Stephens had been arrested, but Ipswich was still deserted at night. A local woman told this author: 'We just weren't sure. It sounds terrible, but we really hoped it was him [Stephens]. We just wanted him off the streets. We wanted to breathe again.'

As Ipswich collectively held its breath, a bunch of weather-beaten roses tied to a lamp post in Ipswich's red light district rustled in the wind; the note could just be made out: 'Tania, Gemma, Netty, Paula, Anni, I knew some of you better than others. But I miss you all. X Tom.'

With Tom Stephens in custody and the police still looking at some strong suspects, the people of Ipswich could still not relax. It was encouraging that there were now some developments in the manhunt, but there was still nothing concrete.

There remained a handful of women working on the streets of the red light district, perhaps six or seven who needed the money that badly. But they were being much more cautious and the police presence was very visible now. It is perhaps significant that none of the women thought that Tom Stephens was the killer. One said: 'It's not him. No way. He's just Tom. He would rather help them than kill them.' However, there was much surprise among the working girls that Stephens had been a special constable.

On 18 December the Ipswich *Evening Star* reported that the media presence in the town had doubled. Along with the broadcast vans equipped with satellite dishes and the catering trucks supplied by PR Catering in Ipswich at the request of the police, Sky News had a team of twenty-five on the scene, along with their own helicopter. Every hotel and bed and breakfast in the town was fully booked by the media. The locals on the other hand were much more low profile during this period, especially after dark, and at this time of the year just a week before Christmas darkness was falling by 4.30pm.

There were some rewards being offered for the information that led to the capture of the killer. A local businessman, Graeme Kaibraier, who ran a call centre in Ipswich, had put up a reward of twenty-five thousand pounds and then doubled it to fifty thousand pounds. He said: 'I have a teenage daughter aged seventeen. I also have an Ipswich workforce of 300, many of whom are girls in their teens and early twenties. I want this killer off the streets.' Meanwhile, the *News of the World* newspaper had offered its own reward of two hundred and fifty thousand pounds.

The media was reporting on many small possible leads too. A barn in the village of Washbrook, less than a mile (1.6km) from both Copdock Mill and Hintlesham, was rumoured to be where the women were killed. This was mainly because prostitutes had taken clients there in the past; in such a jumpy climate it takes very little to fuel speculation.

One theory was that the Ipswich murders had been committed in a copycat style from a crime novel. The book *Devices and Desires*, published by P.D. James in 1989, has a plot that sees five women strangled and their bodies dumped in rural East Anglia, which is geographically close to Suffolk. However, only one of the five women in the book was a prostitute.

For the police, the inquiry had never been more high-powered. The arrest of Tom Stephens had galvanised the media, but on the ground the inquiry was looking at other leads too. Stephens was just one part of the investigation. And the cautious and unexcited tone used by the police when talking about Stephens did not lead any discerning observer to believe that the streets were now safe. Nobody truly knew if Stephens was the killer, an accomplice, just knew something, or was entirely innocent. There had been no emotional closure or relief for the families of the victims, the people of Ipswich or the wider public.

All eyes were on Ipswich, and as the winter winds

chilled the air everybody waited for another development
– for Stephens to be charged, another arrest to be made, or
the worst eventuality – the finding of a sixth body. There
was not too long to wait.

CHAPTER SIX

UNMASKING
THE KILLER

The cold wind that bristled through Ipswich and whistled through the surrounding woodland, rippling the streams and brushing the grass should have carried with it the happy sounds of festive chatter with less than a week to go before Christmas Day. The talk in the shops, streets and alleyways ought to have been of the coming holiday, which had already begun for local children. But the thick and clinging mist of breathless tension continued to hover in the Suffolk air. Nobody could touch it, see it, taste it or hear it. But everybody could feel it.

No further bodies had been discovered for a week. The local people were saving the breath that they had left for developments regarding Tom Stephens. It was far from a feeling of total relief. The breathtaking events that had imposed themselves on the town required much more than an arrest for reassurance. Five families had been struck down by the most painful grief. Everybody waited, and outside of Ipswich the general population of Britain and people even further afield needed final closure, if there could ever be such a thing.

There was not long to wait. Less than twenty-four hours after the arrest of Tom Stephens there was such a development. It was not out in the countryside or in another town. It came from Ipswich itself. Perhaps just a few hundred metres from where the five victims had worked the streets. It was a new day, a new dawn, but for somebody it was the beginning of the end.

TUESDAY, 19 DECEMBER 2006
IPSWICH
5.00am

London Road can be found in the north-west of Ipswich town centre, just north of the Ipswich Town football ground at Portman Road. It lies in the vicinity of the red light district and connects with Handford Road and then merges into the A1214, which is also called London Road, and leads south-west out of Ipswich, joining the A12 and A14 roads. It is a road that is right on the cusp of the town centre itself, but is also one of the major routes in and out of Ipswich as well.

This is a part of the town that is in need of some regeneration and has a rather faded atmosphere. Past a long parade of shops of a random and ramshackle variety, a quick turn to the left brings into view St Matthew's Church; London Road leads on from this. London Road is as winding as it is long; a residential area, the houses appear in many shapes, sizes and styles and date from different periods. In the middle of the day it is almost eerily quiet despite the frequent passing of cars.

Pensioners can be seen pulling their trolleys and

Steven Wright, the man behind the cold blooded murder of five young women.

© *Jason Bye/REX Features; Albanpix Ltd/REX Features*

Above: The families of the victims arrive at Ipswich Crown Court, 22 January 2008.

Below: Inside the home of Steven Wright.

Above left: Pamela Wright, the former partner of Steven Wright.

Above right: Dr Nat Carey, Home Office Pathologist, arriving at court to give evidence.

Below left: Detective Chief Superintendent Stewart Gull.

Below right: Peter Wright QC.

Above: The jury was taken on an official visit to the murder scenes, in and around Ipswich. Here they wend their way towards where Anneli Alderton's body was found, at Nacton.

Below: Flowers marking the spot, near Hintlesham Fisheries, where Gemma Adams body was found.

carrying shopping bags from the town centre; a mother cradles a baby in a doorway, watching the world go by. The sound of daytime television can be heard coming from many of the houses. It is a mixture of council and private accommodation and of houses, flats, bedsits and lodging rooms. The predominant colour is grey, but on the very early morning of 19 December at 5am the road was still in darkness.

A convoy of cars and vans made its way down London Road in the dawn. The vehicles were full of police officers and a forensic team. They had been briefed meticulously and were well prepared for the coming events.

The target was No. 79 London Road. An end-of-terrace Victorian house, it is divided into flats. Typical of the surrounding houses, the front door is to the left on the attached side, with a small window upstairs above the door and a large window to the right of the door at ground level. There is a small driveway to the right of the house and a car park at the back. There is also access to No. 79 through patio doors at the rear of the house. The houses in this stretch of London Road are fairly crammed together and the neighbours have little choice but to notice what goes on around them.

It was one of the flats at No. 79 that the police were focusing their attention on. Dozens of police officers surrounded the house as some began hammering on the door at the front. As soon as the door was opened the officers swarmed into the property.

Minutes later a man was led out in handcuffs, wearing pyjamas and a dressing gown. He was about 6 ft (1.82m) tall with a stocky build and grey, closely cropped hair. He seemed quite composed as he was taken away by officers.

Some neighbours were woken up by the commotion and they could scarcely believe what they were seeing. The forensic team, wearing white protective suits, began making a fingertip search of the house. During the day scaffolding was erected in the driveway of the house, which was to act as the frame for a large white tent used to screen the door from public view.

A car belonging to the arrested man was soon seized. It was a navy blue Ford Mondeo, registration number BO51 CKC. It was later discovered that the car was leased. Forensic tests were conducted on the boot of the car to determine if any bodies had been carried within it. The car was then taken away on a low-loader lorry.

Other officers then began making door-to-door enquiries in London Road and No. 79 was set to be a hive of police activity for days to come.

It had all happened so fast that it was almost impossible to take in. Tom Stephens was still in custody and being questioned. Just as with Stephens, by the end of the day the media had named the second man arrested in the inquiry. Again the police remained silent as the man had not yet been formally charged with anything.

The man arrested at 79 London Road was named as Steven Wright. He was forty-eight years old.

Steven Gerald James Wright was born on 24 April 1958 in Erpingham, Norfolk. The village of Erpingham is situated about 3 miles (4.8km) from Aylsham and was given its name by the family of Sir Thomas Erpingham who lived there for many generations.

Steven was brought up at RAF West Beckham. His father Conrad was a corporal in the RAF and he lived with

Steven's mother Patricia on the base. There were four children, two boys and two girls. It was a typical forces family, where the career of one of the parents dictates the family's lifestyle, living on or near bases and moving to new postings when required. For a period Conrad was posted abroad and the family went with him.

Steven was a shy child but not extraordinary in any way. He was never in trouble with the police and there were no overt signs that he would get into trouble later. Perhaps the most that can be said that is that as an adult he was an impulsive character with a short attention span, resulting in a transient work history and lifestyle. This dominant character trait must have developed in childhood.

In 1977 Conrad and Patricia divorced and Conrad remarried. He and his new wife Valerie moved to the port town of Felixstowe, not far from Ipswich, and Conrad became a docks policeman for the Felixstowe Port Authority. It has been reported that the children did not get on well with Valerie and therefore grew apart from Conrad at this stage. They stayed with their mother Patricia, who had also met a new partner.

In 1978 Steven Wright met and married Angela O'Donovan in a ceremony in West Wales. This marriage would produce three children and they lived in Wales. The children are Anne Marie, aged twenty-two at the time of her father's arrest, George, aged twenty-one, and Dawn, nineteen.

From 1982 Steven Wright began working as a steward on the luxury QE2 (Queen Elizabeth II) cruise liner. This entailed long stretches away from home and cannot have been good for the marriage. It caused a sensation in the media when it was discovered that during this period in Wright's life he had known and worked alongside another crewmember who later vanished and was presumed murdered.

Suzy Lamplugh was twenty-five years old when she vanished in West London in July 1986. She had previously worked as a beautician on the QE2 cruise liner, but at the time of her disappearance she was working as an estate agent. On the day that she went missing Suzy went to show a house to a potential buyer, something that formed an everyday part of her job. The house was in Fulham, south-west London and the appointments book in her office listed the appointment as with a 'Mr Kipper'. Almost immediately, the police became fairly certain that this was a fictitious name and a man of that name was never traced.

The house was thoroughly searched and Suzy Lamplugh's background and associations were painstakingly investigated. But nothing could be found, despite a large-scale police hunt and massive media interest. Suzy's body was never found and eight years later in 1994 she was declared dead, assumed murdered. In 1989 the convicted rapist and murderer John Cannan was arrested in connection with Suzy's disappearance, but no evidence could be found to connect him to the crime.

Steven Wright was never implicated in any way in Suzy's disappearance, but his connection with her on the QE2 now led the media to zero in on this aspect of his past.

In interviews in the *Sun* on 21 December, two days after Wright's arrest, other crewmembers who had worked with both Wright and Lamplugh on the ship spoke out. Whilst these comments should be read objectively, they do give us insights into Steven Wright's character.

It must also be remembered that Wright and Lamplugh did not work directly side by side. He was a steward mainly serving first-class passengers in the ship's Columbia restaurant, while she was a beautician. But they certainly knew each other.

Former QE2 crewmember Steve Adler said about Wright:

'He would sniff around all the girls and particularly the beauticians such as Suzy. There were 900 male crew and 100 female crew on board so the competition for girls was pretty fierce. But Steve put himself around and got a few girlfriends.'

This is perhaps not unusual behaviour for a healthy young man in this situation with long weeks on board. But there seems to have been a seamier side to Wright's behaviour, one that hints that he was something of a loner at times.

Steve Adler continued:

'When we were in Pattaya in Thailand one time we went ashore and found a bar to get drunk in. But Steve was more interested in prostitutes and got himself one. If you went with a hooker, the golden rule was to tell someone, so if you went missing we knew who had gone with who – and we could go and look for them. But Steve would just disappear and never tell a soul.'

It was to emerge that Steve Wright was a frequent patron of prostitutes in later years. Was his time on the QE2 when the habit began to form or had it begun even earlier?

Another former shipmate, who preferred not to be named, said:

'Steve knew Suzy pretty well. Mind you, she was gorgeous and everyone wanted to know her. She had a boyfriend on board and I heard there may have been others. Suzy was the life and soul and everyone wanted to be with her. Steve knew Suzy and she knew him. Everybody mixed with everyone.'

The mere fact that Wright knew Suzy Lamplugh makes him guilty of nothing of course. In such an environment, where men outnumbered women nine to one, attractive females would have been the centre of attention. Steven Wright was perhaps no different from the other male crewmembers in this respect, despite the fact that he was married.

A former QE2 waiter called Paul Tennant said: 'Steve tried to become a friend of Suzy's all the time. Everybody got on with each other in the crew bars, whether it was the "Hatch" where Suzy served drinks, or in the "Pig and Whistle" where we all drank. It was a great shock when Suzy was abducted. I've no idea if Steve and Suzy kept in touch after she left the ship.'

It is striking that Steve Wright knew a young woman who was later to become almost certainly the victim of murder, and that twenty years later Wright himself should be arrested for the suspected murders of five young women. But we must be careful not to make one plus one equal three.

While Steve Wright was working on the QE2, he also met the woman who was to become his second wife, Diane Cassell, who was working onboard as a window dresser. His marriage to Angela had become strained and they eventually divorced. Their three children stayed with Angela.

After the divorce Wright moved in with his father Conrad and his wife Valerie, who had since had a son together, Keith, Steve's half-brother. Wright stayed with them in Felixstowe for about a year. A neighbour of the family said that Steve was 'a little bit shy in conversation'.

Steve Wright went on to marry Diane Cassell in August 1987 in Braintree, Essex. He was twenty-nine and she was four years older. Although they were in a relationship together, the marriage itself was more for practical purposes than the result of desire. As Diane told the Ipswich *Evening Star* on 21 December, they got married because they had decided to run a pub together and to get the licence from the brewery they had to be married. They were soon given the Ferry Boat Inn in Norwich to run, a pub in the town's red light district. This connection would figure more in the ensuing police investigation and will be detailed later.

Steve and Diane were actually married for less than a year and it was not a happy marriage. Diane said:

'I knew him for seven years, but we were only married for five minutes really. It was a long time ago, and I haven't had anything to do with him for ages. I don't want to say too much, but I will say our marriage wasn't great. It wasn't good and I was glad when it ended. I've been in some scrapes in my time and that was one of them.'

The reasons for Diane's unhappiness and the swift breakdown of the marriage are apparent in Diane's following statement: 'He was "tomming" about basically, and I wouldn't put up with it. I had no say in the matter, he just used to say "I'm going out" and that was that. I was just the dutiful wife who ran the pub.'

Although Diane had not seen Steve for many years, his arrest on suspicion of the murders of five women had made her go through it all again in her mind: 'This news has just totally made me rethink everything. He was going out nightclubbing all the time, but now I'm thinking, was he?'

This is particularly poignant when one remembers that the police were now reinvestigating three Norwich murders between the years 1992 and 2002.

After the end of the marriage Diane was left homeless and she moved back to her hometown of Hartlepool, on Teesside. She changed her name by deed poll to make a fresh start. She is now wheelchair-bound, the result of meningitis, and she still lives in Hartlepool with her partner. She had tried to erase the memory of Steve Wright from her mind, but his arrest had dredged it all up again.

The life of Steve Wright continued in the same transient way in the following years. It was reported that for a time he was the landlord of a pub in Plumstead, south-east London. Between 1997 and 2000 he lived in Felixstowe at Stonelands House, Runnacles Way, and it was reported in the *Mirror* on 20 December that he had worked at the Brook Hotel bar in Felixstowe but that he had allegedly been fired for stealing money, as would later be divulged during court proceedings.

For much of the rest of the time, Wright took temporary contract work in warehouses and factories through employment agencies. He also spent a spell working in a bingo hall. It was while he was working at the bingo hall that Wright met Pamela Goodman.

Pamela, who was married and has a grown-up son called Jamie who works as a chef, became Wright's long-term partner. She would eventually become his common-law wife, adopting his surname. In 2002 when Steve Wright moved to Ipswich they set up home together in a one-bedroom flat in Bell Close, south-central Ipswich. Both Steve and Pamela frequented the Uncle Tom's Cabin pub on nearby Vernon Street, using it as their local, and Wright also used the bookmakers close by on occasion.

Their former neighbour in Bell Close, Steve McDonald, who lived upstairs from their flat, gave an interview the day after Wright's arrest. McDonald said:

> 'He's a quiet bloke and friendly but they were always banging around in the flat and arguing. Other neighbours said they'd had to go and ask them to be quiet because the noise was so bad. I didn't get the impression it was a violent relationship necessarily, but it was certainly fiery.'

Pamela worked a night shift in a call centre on the Ransomes industrial estate for a company that deals with out-of-hours calls for businesses. Ex-neighbour Steve McDonald added that Wright would sometimes drive Pamela to work and bring back prostitutes to the flat while Pamela was out: 'Often when Pam was out we heard the kind of noises that a man and woman make together. I couldn't say for sure that he was having sex, but he was definitely having female visitors. And we guessed he wasn't telling Pam about it.'

Another former neighbour in Bell Close, who did not want to be named, told the *Sun* on 20 December:

'They seemed like very normal people. He would often take his wife to work late at night, and would come home in the early hours of the morning. They were a nice couple. They had the occasional argument and you could see there was some sort of stress in the relationship. But it didn't go beyond heated words.'

In September 2006 Steve and Pamela Wright suddenly moved out of the flat in Bell Close. Ex-neighbour Steve McDonald said: 'I heard them banging around in the early hours and found they were going. I was told they were going to rent somewhere bigger as they'd come into money.'

They had moved from Bell Close, on the outskirts of Ipswich's newly trendy docklands area, to 79 London Road, on the edge of the town's red light district, from where prostitutes would begin to go missing within weeks. Pamela would tell friends that they had moved to London Road because Steve especially wanted a garden and the flat in Bell Close had no outside space. He told Pamela that he was spending his spare time at London Road doing DIY and fixing up the new flat.

Wright had been working as a forklift truck driver at Felixstowe docks on a 2–10pm shift. This was a short commute from Ipswich. He was working under contract for Gateway Recruitment Services. A member of staff at Gateway told the *Sun* on 20 December: 'He was a good worker. He was very polite and turned up to jobs on time. It's a great shock to hear he's been arrested.'

Wright's last known workplace was at Cerro Manganese Bronze (Alloys) in Hadleigh road in west Ipswich. The company refused to make any comment about their former employee when approached. Wright had been a foundry supervisor there, but towards the end of September 2006 Wright stopped work. The reason is not known but it is perhaps not so extraordinary as temporary contract work is notoriously unstable. Besides, they still had Pamela's salary coming in.

It seems that Steve and Pamela kept a low profile in their new home, understandably so since Pamela was working a night shift and so had to sleep in the day during the week. Pamela was not even known by some neighbours to be actually living there. Coming in early in the morning and going out again at night, this is perhaps not so strange. A neighbour who lives behind 79 London Road said to the *Sun* on 20 December:

'I didn't see him very much. Only when he was outside cleaning his car. I've seen a woman there too, but I'm not sure if she lives there. They never introduced themselves when they moved in. They never made any effort to talk to anyone, and he never looked up to say hello. I always thought they were very rude.'

Despite having moved to another part of Ipswich, the couple continued to visit their old local pub, Uncle Tom's

Cabin, at 198 Vernon Street. They were good friends with the landlady Sheila Davis and her partner Eddie Roberts. They spent many enjoyable evenings with them and even went on holiday to Ireland with them in 2004.

On the evening of 19 December, the day of Wright's arrest, Pamela went to the pub in tears. She had not been at home when Wright was arrested as she had been at work. In fact, the police had at first assumed that Wright lived alone when they arrested him. That night Pamela told her friend Sheila Davis that she had left Steve in a police cell, where he was being held on suspicion of carrying out the Ipswich murders. Pamela's whole reaction was one of shock and disbelief. Sheila Davis told the *Guardian*:

'Work gave her a lift to the police station, and she has been with the police talking to them all day before she arrived at the pub. She was very upset. But she said she had spoken to the police and she said she had been able to confirm that none of it was true. I think she feels quite confident now that it's not true. She feels the police believed her.'

It is not surprising that Pamela was in deep shock. Discovering that the partner with whom you share your life intimately is suspected of being a serial killer cannot be easy to take in. Another friend of Pamela who did not want to be named told the *Sun* that Pamela had said to her: 'I'm distraught. I just can't believe it's true. He wouldn't hurt a fly. He's innocent. I'm just feeling so lonely tonight.'

Of course, Pamela was questioned as a potential

witness by the police, but her life had been turned upside down by the events of that morning. The dawn raid on her home and the arrest of her partner of five years and common-law husband had pulled the proverbial carpet from under her feet. It must have seemed that everything she believed in was being was being taken away from her.

The pub that night was besieged by members of the media trying to talk to Pamela, once they had learnt that that was where she had gone and that she had been a regular visitor there with Steve Wright. The landlady Sheila Davis offered her a bed there for the night, but Pamela decided to go somewhere else out of the spotlight. Sheila Davis had only positive insights to make about her friends. She told the *Guardian* on 20 December: 'They are a lovely couple. He is very, very quiet, always immaculately turned out in a polo shirt and trousers, never jeans. She is lovely.'

Another friend of Pamela told the *Mirror*:

'He was a real ladies' man. Very attractive and well dressed. But something always made me feel a bit uncomfortable about Steve because he was a bit smarmy. But the moment he phoned to say he was on his way to pick her up she'd have to be at the door waiting.'

The same friend alleged that Wright liked to gamble: 'All his money went on horses. He's got a bit of a gambling problem. He only allowed Pam money to do the shopping, but she got nothing from him if he was gambling.'

Steve Wright had worked for a time in the past at the

Brook Hotel bar in Felixstowe and a regular there also remembered him: 'Steve was quite popular behind the bar and was always up for a chat – especially with the ladies.'

Wright was a keen golfer and a member of Hintlesham Hall Golf Club, coincidentally not far from where the body of Gemma Adams was found on 2 December at Thorpes Hill, Hintlesham. Wright played golf at competition level and had won several trophies. A club member told the *Sun*:

> 'He always wears immaculate black clothes when he plays. Around twenty years ago he worked as a steward for P&O Ferries. Pam used to tell me his clothes had to be immaculate. She used to love the way he dressed.'

Pamela would tell friends that she was a 'golf widow' because of the amount of time that Steve spent playing golf. They would also visit the Uncle Tom's Cabin pub at weekends, where Steve was described as a quiet man who drank four pints of Carlsberg lager on a typical visit to the pub.

When she spoke to the *Times* on 20 December landlady and friend Sheila Davis said that Wright had got on well with her mother. Meanwhile, a regular drinker at Uncle Tom's Cabin told the *Sun*:

> 'I can't believe he'd have carried out these awful murders. No way in a million years would he have done it. I can't see Steve going with prostitutes or having a secret life. He's just a quiet, normal guy and they are happily married.'

This seemed to be the key question – did Steve Wright have a secret life, hidden from Pamela, his friends at the pub and the golf club? Prostitutes who were interviewed painted a darker picture of Wright.

The frequent media interviewee Lou, a working prostitute in Ipswich, said that Wright was a regular punter. She told the *Mirror* on 20 December:

> 'I'd describe him as a regular customer, someone who has been picking up girls for the last eight months or so. I know he uses lots of different prostitutes but I don't know if they include any of the ones who were murdered.'

Lou, a twenty-eight-year-old heroin addict, said that he would trawl the streets of the red light district in his car, which had now of course been taken away by the police. She continued:

> 'You often see him driving round in his blue Mondeo looking for girls even if he had picked you the night before. He didn't strike me as weird and never gave me any reason to believe I was in danger.'

Lou said that she had last had sex with Steve Wright about three weeks before his arrest. She always charged him the usual rate of forty pounds for full sex. She described how it usually happened:

> 'He'd just pick me up and then park in the car park at the back of his house. Sometimes we'd go in the front door and other times through the patio doors at

the back. He'd take me through the kitchen and then upstairs to the bedroom for sex. He didn't want to talk much. It would just be a discussion about how much, the range of services and whatever he wanted. It was always straight sex – nothing out of the ordinary. The last time I saw him was three weeks ago. He picked me up off the street and took me back for sex.'

Lou added that Wright would appear again looking for sex very soon after fulfilling his urge: 'Then I saw him driving around the area the next night in the Mondeo. He appeared to be looking for other girls to pick up.'

It seems that Wright never picked up anyone in London Road itself, but as it is so close to the main pick-up areas of the red light district he did not have far to go. Lou said: 'It would always be in other roads nearby. I would say he was confident. He never struck me as nervous with the girls. Obviously I'm shocked he's been arrested.'

Lou added that she also knew Tom Stephens, the first man to be arrested in Trimley, who was still being questioned by the police on 20 December. She said that Stephens had been a friend, while Wright was only a customer: 'Tom comes down here and helps us girls. I've only met this other guy [Wright] through business.'

Whilst this picture of Wright is very different from the one sketched by his friends and acquaintances who knew him in his 'respectable' persona, there was far more extreme detail to come. In the *Sun* on 21 December, it was alleged that Wright had been seen in the red light district of Norwich in the 1990s trying to pick up prostitutes wearing a short PVC skirt, high heels and a wig. There was an interview with an ex-prostitute called Tina who had worked in the Norwich red light district from about 1996. She said that Wright was still seen in the area at that time (Wright had lived in Norwich in the late 1980s). Tina said:

'He was very strange. I didn't want to get in a car with him, and most of the girls felt the same. He got narked [angry] when you didn't get in the car. He just sat there with the headlights on and would try to talk you round by offering more money.'

Tina also said that the girls in Norwich would call Wright 'the Soldier' because of his habit of wearing camouflage trousers then. The media would have a field day with this – remembering that Tom Stephens had called himself 'the Bishop' on his MySpace page, some tabloids took to referring to the two arrested men as 'The Bishop and The Soldier'.

These two distinctive versions of Steve Wright are difficult to reconcile as the same man. There was the golfer who sometimes played thirty-six holes in a day, liked a sociable drink in the pub, was quiet and generally well liked by those around him. Was this Dr Jekyll? Then there is the image of Wright the serial prowler for prostitutes, trawling dingy twilit streets for sex, behind his partner Pamela's back while she was at work. Was this Mr Hyde?

It is certainly not impossible for a man to have such a secret life. Many murderers have been able to conceal their terrifying inner world from a partner, family and friends, often for years. And regularly using prostitutes does not mean that Steve Wright is a murderer. Such an assertion takes evidence and the police had to have something on him.

By the morning of 20 December, Steve Wright had slept in a police cell and Pamela was homeless, staying with friends and then in safe houses. The call centre where she worked said that she was not expected back there in the near future. She was in deep shock, as were all the people who knew Steve Wright in Ipswich.

A friend summed it all up in an interview in the *Guardian* on 21 December:

'When I heard what happened, two things went through my mind. I thought he is such a nice, lovely guy he could never do something like that. But then I thought, well, if he did it how come he manages to hide something like that so well? We drink together, play golf together, go on holiday together. It's unbelievable. I've known him for years.'

Steve Wright's father Conrad was just as shocked as Pamela at his son's arrest. The seventy-two-year-old, a former RAF corporal and docks policeman, is retired and still lives in Felixstowe. He had some interesting insights to offer about his son, although he had not seen him since 2001.

Conrad Wright told the *Sun* on 20 December, the day after his son's arrest:

'When I heard there had been an arrest of a forty-eight-year-old man in Ipswich, I actually piped up and said, "Steve's forty-eight and lives in Ipswich." But I never thought it would be him in a million years.'

Conrad said that his son Steve had debts of over forty thousand pounds in unsecured loans, money which he had spent during wild spending sprees. He also commented on the impulsiveness of his son and said that about five years earlier Steve had suddenly sold his car and all of his belongings and gone off to Thailand for a six-week holiday. It should be remembered that Steve Wright had visited Thailand years earlier when he was a steward on the QE2 and that a shipmate said that he had paid for the services of a prostitute on that trip. Conrad said: 'I went round to his place and it was stripped bare. No furniture – he had flogged the lot.'

As already mentioned, Steve had a troubled relationship with Conrad's second wife Valerie, although he had lived with them for a short time. Conrad remembered the last time that Steve had visited them, and the argument that ensued: 'The last time Steve was round years ago, he had a big row with Valerie and hyperventilated and collapsed in the kitchen. I had to call an ambulance.'

This is a very enlightening comment and perhaps suggests that Steve had a problem suppressing and controlling his anger. It would take extreme rage to hyperventilate to the point of requiring an ambulance. If Steve Wright had an anger problem, it has to be relevant to any understanding of his character and his potential actions. Conrad believed in his son's innocence and did not think that he would be able to carry out such extreme and well-planned actions.

Conrad said:

'I don't actually think he's clever enough to commit these crimes. They take a level of intelligence I don't think Steve has. He's just not capable of killing people.'

It was soon apparent that the police considered the arrest of Steve Wright as more important than that of Tom Stephens, who had been taken into detention and continuously questioned the day before Wright. A police source said that Wright's detention was 'a far more significant arrest'.

It emerged that DNA samples had been retrieved from more than one of the five victims and that these had been inputted into the national DNA database. The police had then followed the advice of the Forensic Science Service and arrested Wright.

This meant that a sample of Steve Wright's DNA must have been on the database already or that his DNA must have been obtained in some way. This information was not forthcoming at this stage. The national DNA database is a growing one in Britain as in many other countries, but only a small percentage of citizens currently have their DNA stored there.

The fact that there seemed to be some solid scientific evidence linking him to the victims and crime scenes did not look good for Wright. Since DNA became admissible as evidence in court its importance in gaining convictions in major cases has grown rapidly. Likewise, the speed in which tests can be carried out has increased hugely, from weeks to hours. There had been some controversy not long before this case about the quality of some DNA evidence, specifically evidence relying on only a very tiny speck of DNA. But in the case of Wright and the Ipswich murders there would prove to be enough evidence to connect him to the victims and the sites where their bodies were found. The main contention would prove to be pinpointing when the DNA traces were left there.

As examined earlier, the fact that the first two victims to be found, Gemma Adams and Tania Nicol, had been discovered in water meant that the amount of DNA evidence retrieved was negligible. As a police source said after Wright's arrest:

'The fact the first girls found were in water showed the suspect had forensic awareness. We were puzzled why the last three were found on land. This provided us with a much better opportunity to retrieve evidence. At that point, it seemed almost as if the killer actually wanted to be caught. We recovered DNA at three sites, and this has proved a vital tool in the investigation.'

It seemed highly likely that the DNA had been found at the sites where Anneli Alderton, Paula Clennell and Annette Nicholls had been found on land. But this was yet to be confirmed.

The police were also gathering evidence in other ways, as they needed as much as possible if they were going to be able to charge Wright. On 20 December, the day after his arrest, the police were granted a further thirty-six hours to question him. The police took CCTV footage from Uncle Tom's Cabin and from a CCTV camera situated on London Road where he lived. The surveillance footage from the red light district was also being thoroughly analysed and re-analysed, especially that covering the times the five women were known to have disappeared.

The medical records of Steve Wright were also taken from a doctor's surgery in Felixstowe. Our medical details are highly confidential, but the police do have the right to seize such information when pursuing a serious investigation.

The police search continued at 79 London Road, with the forensic team in their white suits taking the place apart in fingertip searches. Wright's blue Mondeo car was also being microscopically searched at a police facility. Meanwhile, the home of Tom Stephens in Jubilee Close, Trimley was still being searched.

The police were also checking the mobile phone data on phones belonging to Wright and Stephens. They had to rule out the possibility of some sort of collusion between the two. But as a police source told the *Sun*: 'There is no evidence to suggest the two knew each other. But we are trying to find out if they were in contact. Both came into our inquiry separately. It was not information from one leading to the other's arrest.'

Police detectives in Norwich were now re-examining the murders of two prostitutes and the disappearance of a third. They were the murder of sixteen-year-old Natalie Pearman, who was found strangled on the outskirts of Norwich in 1992; Michelle Bettles, twenty-two, who was found strangled in 2002; and twenty-nine-year-old Kellie Pratt, who disappeared from the Norwich red light district in 2000 and whose body was never found.

As already stated, Steve Wright lived in Norwich in the late 1980s and ran a pub, the Ferry Boat Inn, which is in the red light district of the city. The pub was frequented by prostitutes and their clients at the time that Wright and his second wife Diane ran it in 1987–88. Remembering that an ex-prostitute from Norwich had seen Wright in the area as late as 1996, this connection had to be investigated.

Regarding the Ferry Boat Inn itself, there were somewhat spurious claims on the internet alleging that it was a hangout for the right-wing British National Party (BNP), even alleging that Wright was a BNP member himself. There is no evidence to support either claim.

A Norfolk police spokesman said: 'We are continuing to check our database to see if there is any information with the inquiries into prostitutes' murders that have occurred in Norwich over recent years that may assist Suffolk Police with enquiries.'

There was also much attention being given to Wright's leased car, the navy blue Ford Mondeo. There had been many reports earlier during the police inquiry about the importance of a blue BMW seen in the red light district on numerous occasions, and even picking up girls. A crime blog on the internet compared the Ford Mondeo with a BMW 325, displaying pictures of them side by side; the similarities are indeed striking in overall shape and design.

The blog stated on 19 December, the day of Wright's arrest:

'Notice the lines of the car are almost identical. Now imagine that you are seeing this car, from a distance, not still on a webpage, where you have all the time in the world for comparison... Could this have been the car described by police, with only the model being wrong?'

While this is clearly speculation, there is a point. The BMW had been seen fleetingly and usually in the dark and the shade of blue is the same as Wright's Ford Mondeo.

Wright's neighbour in London Road, David Welton, told the media: 'He [Wright] was always cleaning that Mondeo both inside and out.' The blue Ford Mondeo would indeed figure in the case against Steven Wright.

As mentioned in Chapter Four, the police had been in contact with their colleagues in Atlantic City, New Jersey, during their investigations. Four prostitutes had been murdered in Atlantic City, their bodies discovered in a single month, November 2006. In the case of Ipswich five prostitutes had been discovered murdered a month later in December 2006.

Some form of strangulation, asphyxiation and compression to the neck was used in the modus operandi of the killers on both sides of the Atlantic. But according to Eric W. Hickey in his 2006 book *Serial Murderers and their Victims*, strangulation was used in whole or in part in 35 per cent of all serial killer cases in the United States between 1800 and 2004.

The Atlantic City victims were all found in water. In Ipswich this was the case with only two out of five victims. In Atlantic City the women were found fully clothed with only their shoes removed. In Ipswich they were completely naked. There are similarities between the two murder sprees and it is obvious to see why the police investigating the Ipswich murders were talking to their counterparts in Atlantic City. The sharing of methods and ideas could only help both inquiries.

It was reported in the *Sun* on 21 December that Steve Wright was refusing to co-operate with the police and would not answer their questions. A police source said: 'At the moment Wright isn't playing ball with us. He is exercising his right not to answer questions.'

It was also reported that Wright had been put on suicide watch. His father Conrad had said that his son was prone to bouts of depression and the police were taking no chances.

On the evening of Thursday, 21 December, two days after Wright's arrest, Detective Chief Superintendent Stewart Gull made his usual appearance at the Ipswich inquiry's daily press conference. But the media were now desperate for any developments on Steven Wright; the fact that senior prosecutors from the Crown Prosecution Service had arrived at the Suffolk Police headquarters just an hour earlier only increased the tension.

At 10.15pm, Detective Chief Superintendent Stewart Gull stepped up to the microphone and said:

'You will be aware that on Monday, December 18, as part of our investigation into the murders of five women in the Ipswich area, we arrested a suspect at his home address in Trimley. The next day, Tuesday, December 19, a second suspect was arrested in Ipswich. There have been significant ongoing enquiries and interviews during the period that these men have been in custody.

'As a result of these enquiries, the thirty-seven-year-old man from Trimley was this evening released on police bail, pending further enquiries. Police will not name this man at this stage.

'The second man, Steven Wright from Ipswich, has been charged with the murder of all five women.'

The irony was that Tom Stephens had actually been named by the media within hours of his arrest. Stephens was taken to a police safe house, as the police were concerned about the possibility of a vigilante-style attack. Michael Crimp, Senior Prosecutor for the Suffolk Crown Prosecution Service, also made a statement:

'Working as part of a team of lawyers overseen by the Chief Crown Prosecutor for Suffolk, I was briefed on this case prior to any arrests being made and the entire team has kept in close contact with the police throughout. We have been working with officers from Suffolk Constabulary for the last eight days advising on a number of preliminary legal issues both before and after arrest. As this case has developed we have been carefully examining and assessing the evidence in order to come to a charging decision at the earliest possible opportunity. This evening we have made the decision that there is sufficient evidence and authorised that Steven Wright born on the 24 of April 1958 of London Road, Ipswich should be charged with the murder of Tania Nicol, Gemma Adams, Anneli Alderton, Annette Nicholls and Paula Clennell. We will continue to keep this case under constant review as it develops. Mr Wright will be kept in custody to appear before Ipswich Magistrates' Court tomorrow. At this time I would like to remind you of the need to take care in reporting the events surrounding this case. Steven Wright stands accused of these offences and has the right to a fair trial before a jury. It is extremely important that there should be responsible media reporting which should not prejudice the due process of law.'

The arrest of Tom Stephens on the morning of 18 December had already sent the huge media presence in Ipswich into an expectant frenzy and the second arrest of Steven Wright less than twenty-four hours later brought them to fever pitch. With news helicopters flying overhead, outside broadcast and catering vans on the sides of roads around the red light district, the atmosphere was reaching a climax.

The first arrest of Stephens had occurred in the quiet village of Trimley St Martin between Ipswich and Felixstowe, but the arrest of Wright within streets of where the murdered women worked their patch was nothing short of sensational. The local people of Ipswich were shocked by the speed of Wright's arrest so soon after that of Stephens, and by the close proximity of his house to the red light district.

A local shopkeeper working close to the red light area, and just a five-minute walk from Wright's home on London Road, told this author: 'We were surprised initially because the primary suspect came from a village near Felixstowe. When this guy down here was arrested, that came as quite a surprise.'

The feeling was also one of cautious relief. Had a face finally been given to the perpetrator of these cold-blooded acts? Everybody hoped so, but there was still an element of fear amongst the local population and the police that another body would surface and destroy yet another family.

The media apparatus was now in full force on a truly global level; Ipswich was a place now known throughout the developed world. The police public relations team in the town was inundated.

The media presence was somewhat claustrophobic for the local people too. As an elderly local woman told the author: 'We felt hemmed in. We were trying to take in what had happened, but it felt like our little town had been taken over. I've lived here all my life, seventy-three years, and I've never seen anything like it before.'

It must have seemed as if the town was under siege. The main focus of media activity was around the temporary police cabin that had been placed at the junction of London Road and Handford Road; in addition there were media crews camped outside the homes of Tom Stephens and Steven Wright. When it was learnt that Wright's arrest was considered far more significant, television crews stationed themselves just outside the police cordon on London Road. The effect on local residents was suffocating.

In the late twentieth- and early twenty-first centuries, the media has been and will continue to be a key player in any high-profile murder case. Looking back throughout history we can see that such intense attention has been evident as far back as the Jack the Ripper murders in London in the autumn of 1888, and in Dr Crippen's transatlantic capture and trial in 1912. In the twentieth century the media spotlight followed the Moors murders and the case of Bible John in Scotland in the 1960s; the Yorkshire Ripper in the 1970s; the Jeremy Bamber case and the Hungerford massacre of the 1980s; Dr Shipman and Fred and Rose West in the 1990s. Now there were the Soham murders, the Ipswich murders and the Madeleine McCann abduction case in the first decade of the new century. And these are only the British cases (or those involving Britons) that have had a global impact.

The way that a modern police force handles the media through public relations has never been more crucial. An inquiry on the scale of the Ipswich murders is reliant on the media for appeals for information primarily, but the way that the inquiry is reported is also very important, as made clear by the statement issued by the Crown Prosecution service after the charging of Wright and the bailing of Stephens. Aside from any legal considerations, when a police force is under tremendous pressure to get a result, the way the case is reported can heighten or ease the pressure on those in the front line of the inquiry.

The media reporting of the police handling of the Ipswich inquiry was largely sympathetic and supportive, reflecting the professional and focused way in which the case was dealt with, despite the most enormous pressure. But there was some criticism levelled at the media itself, especially the tabloid newspapers, by the people of Ipswich, concerning the intrusive and unsympathetic way in which some of the developments were reported. Likewise, there was understandable concern in legal and police circles that Tom Stephens and Steven Wright were named by the media within hours of their arrests and before either was charged.

In the case of Wright, in one sense this premature exposure turned out not to be so serious, as he did go on to be charged and therefore publicly named. Nevertheless the intensive reporting on Wright between his arrest and charging two-and-a-half days later had the potential to prejudice his trial, as it would have been difficult to find a jury that had not been exposed to this media onslaught of information. This would become a key component of Wright's defence.

One interesting aspect of the media reporting on Tom Stephens was the reliance on the loner or misfit stereotype. The media likes nothing more than to unveil a monster whose habits or actions deviate from those considered socially 'normal' by the majority of people. When this is attached to a convicted killer, it poses little problem, but when somebody is arrested and not yet charged with any crime, it can be very damaging to the individual concerned – not to mention the whole inquiry. The fact that Stephens had to be taken to a police safe house because of fears of a vigilante attack illustrates this.

As seen in Chapter Five, Tom Stephens had put himself in the media spotlight through his own free will and on one level he may even have enjoyed being the centre of attention. But any individual is owed a duty of care by the media. The BBC was perhaps rightly criticised for publicly releasing the interview that Stephens gave to the reporter Trudi Barber. There had allegedly been an agreement between the reporter and Stephens that the interview would be used only for background or 'local colour' purposes. Instead the details of it were released after Stephens' arrest.

The media reflects the public's interests and perceptions in its mission to sell newspapers and generate television ratings; in turn it creates and confirms those interests and perceptions. The media and public branding of the killer type is very widespread. There seems no doubt that all premeditated killers are abnormal in some way, but this abnormality is often not clearly visible. In reality the killer might not be the person with unconventional looks or habits but instead an all-smiling family man, an upstanding or at least an accepted member of society.

This over-simplification of the misfit stereotype

becomes a real problem when it influences a jury or wider public perception. Thankfully, advances in DNA fingerprinting and analysis – pioneered by Alec Jeffreys in 1986 – have meant that the perceived character of the accused is no longer so fundamental to the case. As the leading crime writer Colin Wilson has said: 'Genetic fingerprinting was perhaps the most important innovation in crime detection since digital fingerprinting in the 1880s.' The use of DNA evidence was proving to be absolutely crucial to the Ipswich inquiry.

At worst, media-fuelled stereotypes can lead to miscarriages of justice. If the public have a preconceived idea of what a killer, particularly a sexually motivated one, looks or behaves like, it can cloud judgements – of a jury, or even of the police if they are under pressure to get a conviction. The following tragic case illustrates this.

On 12 November 2006, a fifty-four-year-old comic book dealer called Ronald Castree was jailed for life for the murder of eleven-year-old Lesley Molseed, more than thirty years earlier in 1975. The little girl had been sexually assaulted and stabbed twelve times in a frenzied attack before her body was dumped on nearby moors. Castree was living on the same housing estate as Lesley Molseed at the time and had no alibi. Castree was twenty-two. However, another local man in Rochdale, Stefan Kiszko, was soon arrested for the murder. Kiszko was a big, gentle man who some would have described as a loner. All of his family and neighbours considered him innocent. The key evidence against Kiszko came from three teenage girls who said that Kiszko had stalked them and exposed himself to them. Kiszko, a tax clerk, was tried and sent to prison for life.

Kiszko had already served sixteen years in prison when he was granted an appeal. Lesley's underwear had been carefully stored as forensic evidence and DNA tests exonerated Kiszko. In fact Kiszko had always been infertile and tests carried out in 1975 proved this; he could therefore never have left the semen stains on Lesley's knickers. But this evidence had not been put forward to the original trial jury.

Stefan Kiszko was duly released in 1992 and given a fulsome apology from the police and the original trial judge. The three teenage girls were found and re-interviewed and they admitted making up the stalking and flashing story 'for a laugh'.

Sadly Kiszko was now something of a broken man and had developed schizophrenia in prison. He died a recluse within two years of his release and exoneration.

Meanwhile Ronald Castree had prospered in his comic business and was the father of two. His family had no idea of his guilt. But in 2005 his DNA sample was taken in connection with a sexual attack on a woman in Oldham, and his swab was a perfect match for the DNA taken from Lesley Molseed's underwear.

The West Yorkshire Police, who had led the inquiry into Ronald Castree, made a public statement. A senior policeman said: 'We are very, very sorry for what happened. It was a dreadful miscarriage of justice.'

From the moment that Detective Chief Superintendent Stewart Gull announced the charging of Steve Wright on the night of 21 December there was a media blackout; all reporting on the Ipswich murders inquiry and Steven Wright himself was suspended while the case was *sub judice.* Only reporting on the facts from trial proceedings was allowed, the normal procedure once a suspect has been charged.

This was perhaps just as well. On 19 December, the Ipswich *Evening Star* carried an article about rogue media reporting in the town. Some foreign journalists had tried to get into the mortuary of Ipswich Hospital where the bodies of the five murdered women were located.

On 21 December, the same newspaper's front page was headlined 'Britain's Saddest TV Star'. It was the story of Lou, the Ipswich prostitute and heroin addict who had become such a staple media interviewee over the recent weeks.

In the same issue the police were reported as becoming increasingly concerned about media coverage. After all the pressure and emotional trauma of those weeks running up to Christmas they were understandably worried that unscrupulous reporting might have an impact on the police case.

This was a view shared by many in Ipswich. A local shopkeeper told this author: 'The worry is that something has been said which will prejudice the case...and that an evil man actually gets let out on a technicality. It's actually got nothing to do with justice – a lawyer who supports one side might try to put one over on a colleague, sometimes from the same chambers on the other side, rather than everyone pulling together to get justice.'

The day after Steven Wright was charged with the murders of all five women, he appeared at Ipswich Magistrates Court. He arrived there at 9.26am, wearing a suit bought for him by the police to wear to his court appearances. He had travelled there in a metal cage inside a police van, surrounded by a police escort of two motorcycle outriders and three Volvo estate cars. He spoke only to confirm his name and had a blanket over his head to shield him from waiting photographers and television cameras. He was remanded in custody until 2 January 2007. When he returned to Ipswich Magistrates Court on that date he was remanded in custody until 1 May.

Meanwhile, on the day that Wright made his first court appearance, the father of Tom Stephens, Douglas Stephens, told the media that he had spoken to his son on the telephone, and that Tom was 'perfectly calm'. Still in a safe house, he was apologetic for what he had put his parents through, but he was pleased to have been bailed.

After leaving the court on 22 December, Steve Wright was transferred to Belmarsh Prison in south-east London, a high security prison often used to hold defendants in high-profile cases while awaiting trial. He was taken south down the motorway in a white police van with reinforced doors and windows, sandwiched by a police escort.

Wright was immediately put in a cell in the high-security prison that had been specially designed to prevent prisoner suicides. The cell has a reinforced glass door and a special design to prevent hanging attempts. The furniture is made of reinforced plastic and two or three prison officers were assigned to watch Wright twenty-four hours a day.

The special cell is in the healthcare wing of the prison and was last used to hold Ian Huntley in 2003. He was awaiting trial for the Soham murders, which saw him convicted and sentenced to life in prison for the murders of the two schoolgirls Holly Wells and Jessica Chapman.

The placing of such defendants in suicide-proof cells

has been adopted in recent years because of controversial suicides of prisoners, namely the convicted murderers Fred West and Dr Harold Shipman, both of whom hanged themselves in their cells. The fact that the cell Wright was in had not been used since Ian Huntley three years earlier demonstrates how much of a suicide risk the authorities considered him to be.

As we saw, his father Conrad was concerned that Steve might attempt suicide. It emerged that Wright's common-law wife Pamela also feared the same. Since just after the arrest, Pamela had been staying in a succession of police safe houses. In an interview in the *Sunday Telegraph* on 24 December, a close friend of Pamela, Patrick Keohane, said: 'She just wants to speak to him, but the police say she can't at the moment. She told me, "He's such a quiet bloke, he won't be able to take it." I had to tell her that he won't be able to do anything to himself because they will be watching over him twenty-four hours a day.'

According to Mr Keohane, who was consoling Pamela, she was now on tranquillisers. The fact that Wright had been charged had deeply shocked her as she had thought he would be released. He said: 'She can't eat without feeling sick. We have tried giving her brandy to make her sleep. It doesn't really work. She can only manage about two hours. She's been in a dreadful state.'

Mr Keohane also said that although Pamela felt that Steve would eventually be cleared, she already understood that they would never be able to resume their old life together. Mr Keohane said: 'She has already talked about getting their stuff together and moving away.'

Sheila Davis, a friend of both Pamela and Steve and landlady of the Uncle Tom's Cabin pub, said: 'This has destroyed her life. She hasn't got a job because she feels too devastated to go back to work. She hasn't got a home because the police are there. She feels she has lost everything.'

Wright's legal team, which would change over the coming months, was also concerned that it might be impossible for him to get a fair trial. His first lawyer, Paul Osler, said that the legal team would begin examining the extensive media coverage over the Christmas holiday. Osler hoped that it might be possible to get Wright released if he could show that media reports had prejudiced the case. Mr Osler said: 'We will be looking at it all. Defence lawyers will look to see if an argument should be put before the court that the prosecution has become an abuse of process because there can no longer be a fair trial.'

Steve Wright never got bailed and he would stay in his special cell at Belmarsh Prison until his main trial began.

The fact that unscrupulous media reporting was going to form part of the basis for Wright's defence strategy was becoming obvious. The then Chief Constable of Suffolk, Alastair McWhirter, and the Attorney General, Lord Goldsmith, had both now appealed to the media to show restraint in the reporting of the Ipswich inquiry.

Eminent lawyers were also beginning to voice their concerns that media coverage was leading to a state in which a defendant's right to a fair trial was in jeopardy, undermining one of the founding principles of the democratic justice system.

A leading barrister, Christopher Sallon QC, who had recently defended a murder defendant in a high-profile case, said: 'The slow inroads being made into the

Contempt of Court Act are critically undermining of the justice system in this country. The Attorney General should initiate an inquiry and look at what has been said and the impact that it could have. And he should consider proceedings if he thinks it appropriate.' The Ipswich inquiry was now making significant legal waves. This would continue to have a large bearing on the legal proceedings against and for Steven Wright.

As Christmas passed and 2006 gave way to 2007 no new bodies were discovered in Ipswich. There had been a fear that a further body might be found in the vicinity of where Anneli Alderton was found, as the other four women seemed to have been found in pairs. This might have led some people to think that the killer was off the streets as the murders had ceased, but this of course is no guarantee of anything. There have been other cases of cunning serial killers going to ground once somebody else has been charged.

Steve Wright sat in his specially designed cell, solitary and with twenty-four hours a day to ponder his future. Only he knew the truth at this stage. The five other people who knew what had happened could not bear witness, but their traumatised families deserved to know the truth. As the legal machinery swung into operation and both the prosecution and defence teams began building their cases, some calm returned to Ipswich, but it was a both a weary and wary calm. Some innocence had been lost. But the community had withstood an enormous test.

CHAPTER SEVEN

THE QUEST FOR JUSTICE

Steven Wright appeared at Ipswich Magistrates' Court, situated between the railway station and the Portman Road football ground, on 1 May 2007. Ironically it is just a short walking distance from his last home where he was arrested and from the town's red light district where the five murdered women had worked the streets.

His case was heard in Court 1 and the hearing began at 2pm. The judge presiding was the Honourable Mr Justice Calvert-Smith, and it was a preliminary hearing looking at aspects of plea and case management. In essence it was to ascertain the progress of the prosecution case, to listen to any concerns from both legal sides, and to set a date for the trial.

The prosecution team was led by Peter Wright QC – who by coincidence shared the same surname as the man he was prosecuting. He had previously prosecuted the most prolific serial killer in British history, Dr Harold Shipman, in 1999. He was supported by Simon Spence.

Wright's defence team was led by the very experienced Timothy Langdale QC, who had successfully defended the Birmingham Six (wrongly convicted of a 1970s IRA pub bombing in Birmingham) in their final appeal. He was backed up by Neil Saunders.

Outside the court there was a great media presence, with dozens of television crews and journalists. But there were only a few members of the public. It had been over five months since Wright's arrest.

Inside the court were members of three of the five victims' families, those of Gemma Adams, Paula Clennell and Tania Nicol. They sat just a few feet from Wright in the dock, in the space usually reserved for a jury. The father of the defendant, Conrad Wright, sat in the public gallery. Several senior officers represented the Suffolk Police, including Detective Chief Superintendent Stewart Gull, who had led the Ipswich inquiry.

Only eleven media organisations were permitted in the main court. Forty other journalists and writers (including this author) were accommodated in a specially designated annex watching by video link. Wright had arrived hours earlier at 9am, in an effort to avoid the media glare. He had been woken in his cell at Belmarsh at 5.30am, and had left for Ipswich at 6.30am. He was wearing a black suit, white shirt and a blue tie.

The plea came first and, as expected, Wright answered 'Not guilty' to all five counts of murder against Gemma Adams, Tania Nicol, Anneli Alderton, Paula Clennell and Annette Nicholls.

Then there were amendments to the indictment, proposed by the defence. Two references were asked to be amended: 'contrary to common law' to be deleted, and 'particular day' to be changed to 'on a day'. Also, Wright wanted to be referred to as 'Steve' rather than 'Steven'. The judge did not object to any of these changes.

The defence then put forward its views in regard to case management. Timothy Langdale QC made an application for a change of venue, and at length laid out his case in support of this. He said that the case was 'exceptional in terms of the nature of the crimes alleged'.

He cited 'the widespread and sensationalist media coverage' and 'the comment on the accused before this trial'. He went on to quote the Legal Procedure Act, Section 41, related to 'no reporting of the arguments'. He said: 'Common sense and experience show that there is a significantly high risk of prejudice in a trial like this.'

He alluded to 'bias, prejudice and inflamed emotions' in the local area and that 'risk should not be run in the interests of justice'. Langdale then listed examples where trials had benefited from more neutral locations: those of Ian Huntley, Dr Harold Shipman, Rosemary West, Peter Sutcliffe and Michael Stone, all of which were eventually relocated.

He mentioned local sensitivity and the supposed links to other unsolved murders in the area, and Mr Langdale pointed out that the 'sensational media allegations touch upon Mr Wright personally'. He then brought up the fact that the Crown Prosecution Service and the Attorney General 'saw fit to give a warning about the nature of reporting' in relation to the case. This was a unique event, he said.

He went on to talk about the effect on a local jury, and that the impact on the daily lives of local people had been large. But he added that a jury drawn from the wider area of Suffolk rather than Ipswich was not a viable option because of 'the risk of contact with local people'.

He next focused on Tom Stephens, saying that Stephens 'needs very special care' and that 'any interference with witnesses would impact on the defendant's welfare', and supported this by saying that there was a fear of vigilante attack when Stephens was released. Moving on to more general problems with influences on potential jurors, he said that 'potential jurors might have had dealings with Ipswich prostitutes and massage parlours'.

Next he pointed to the public displays of emotion, mourning and support, and that the 'Somebody's Daughter' charity campaign was at one stage attracting donations of a thousand pounds a day. He said that the events 'registered more with the local area than it would nationally' and that the 'strength of local feeling would be very difficult to neutralise by direction'.

Finally, Mr Langdale concluded for the defence, saying that the logistics of Wright travelling from Belmarsh in south-east London to Ipswich every day for the duration of the trial would be too much. It was a five-hour round trip and 'the pressure on Wright would be enormous'.

Then it was the turn of the prosecution. Peter Wright QC first cited that the defence had sought to exclude Anneli Alderton from any connection with Ipswich, saying that she only worked there. He said that the prosecution denied this and that Anneli Alderton 'had many convictions in Ipswich', the last one being in 2005 for 'drugs or some form of dishonesty'.

Peter Wright QC then stated that the trial would last between six to eight weeks. The judge expressed concern about this length of time, making a reference to the

176

Yorkshire Ripper Peter Sutcliffe, and that Wright was not claiming to be 'mad' as Sutcliffe had. Mr Justice Calvert-Smith added that he had 'faith in the jurors aquitting themselves well'.

Peter Wright QC said that the 'reliability of scientific evidence is at the core of this case'. He continued with his assertion that there was neither a 'baying crowd' nor 'mass popular dissent' against Steve Wright. He went on to say that if the venue could not be changed, could Wright be moved to either Norwich or Chelmsford high-security prisons for the duration of the trial?

He added that Tom Stephens 'may eventually have a bearing on things', and the judge agreed that 'Stephens is bound to feature somehow'. Peter Wright followed by saying: 'It is the Crown's view that it is not certain that all five murders were committed by a single person' and that 'they may indeed have been committed by more than one hand.' Justice Calvert-Smith said that 'the full scale of the case is not immediately apparent' and that it might be subject to review later.

Peter Wright then said that there had been restrained reporting locally, and made a reference to the 'lurid aspects' of the national tabloid press, and that an 'absence of lurid interest is required' in this case. He cited the national coverage as alleging that Wright was a user of prostitutes, that he had been sacked from a previous job, and that he was a ladies' man. However, he added that some people had come forward to say that Steve Wright 'wasn't the sort of person to do this sort of thing'. He ended by saying that 'the time around these events could be described as a community crisis'.

Justice Calvert-Smith then began his summing up. He

said: 'The basic principle is that cases should be tried in the locality of where the offences are committed. It will be possible to find a jury in this locality. This case should stay in Suffolk and be tried by a Suffolk jury.'

The Ruling was then made official: the trial would take place in Suffolk. Peter Wright QC then said: 'It is unlikely that the case will be ready for trial until the New Year.' He went on to propose a start date of 14 January, and that the trial would last from six to eight weeks.

Judge Calvert-Smith said: '14 January can be more or less set in stone. It will happen on 14 January, even if it happens somewhere else.'

It was then left to discuss the case preparation and the complex logistics involved. Peter Wright said that there was 'much scientific work to be done' and specifically that there was 'quite a bit of fibre work still to be done'. The judge set the completion date for fibre work as 31 July 2007. The pathology report from Dr Nat Carey was due on that date also. Apparently Dr Carey, a Home Office pathologist, was concerned about the toxicology and DNA evidence, as it was crucial.

The deadline for DNA and DNA profiling was set for 31 May, and that for hair analysis set for 17 May. The toxicology report and the CCTV evidence (which was still being gathered) were given a provisional delivery date of the end of May 2007.

Peter Wright said that there would be visual presentations of scientific evidence and location plans as well as photographs of crime scenes. He added that the key analysis would be focused on the five crime sites, Steve Wright's car and his clothing.

The prosecution then said that a particular witness

would not be called as ongoing legal matters would 'throw up many satellite issues'. The witness was possibly unreliable, and credibility might be affected. But Peter Wright QC added that it was not the intention of the prosecution to use 'bad character' attacks on prostitute evidence and witnesses.

Steve Wright had sat emotionless throughout the proceedings, with his head bowed for much of the time. There were also no emotional outbursts from anybody within the court. It was carried out in a dignified and reverent silence.

But as Steve Wright was driven back to Belmarsh Prison in the dark, in his metal cage in the back of the reinforced police van, his head must have been spinning. He faced another eight-and-a-half months in his special cell before the trial even started.

As planned, the trial of Steve Wright began on 14 January 2008. He had been held in Belmarsh for all of the time awaiting trial and was moved to a high-security prison much closer to Ipswich just before his trial began. The trial did indeed take place at Ipswich Crown Court, and early that morning the media focus was once again on Ipswich.

Some members of the media had taken up position outside the court as early as 6am. It was a cold and windy day, and there was a media area specially built outside the court to accommodate the journalists, cameras and photographers. Other media representatives were penned in by metal police barriers. One television cameraman was using an aerial platform about 60ft (18.3m) above Russell Road to get footage of Wright arriving. Higher in the sky itself were helicopters belonging to the Suffolk Police, keeping an eye on events, as well as the BBC and Sky helicopters. Conversely, there were few members of the public outside the court. Police officers wearing fluorescent jackets guarded the court entrance.

At 9.12am, Steve Wright arrived in a white prison van with a police escort; the camera flashes were blinding. There were some spaces in the public gallery, which holds just eighteen people, but those were largely filled by the media. There was also a special annex again, and journalists and writers (including the author) watched from this vantage point. Steve Wright's father Conrad and his brother-in-law Keith were in court too, and they sat in another annex. None of the families of the victims attended on the opening day.

The trial judge was the Honourable Mr Justice Gross (Sir Peter Gross), who was knighted in 2001, the year after he became a High Court judge on the Queen's Bench Division. He had also been the presiding judge on the South Eastern Circuit since 2004. Educated at the University of Cape Town, South Africa, before being awarded a Rhodes Scholarship to Oriel College, Oxford, he was called to the Bar, Gray's Inn, in 1977, became a QC in 1992, and a Recorder in 1995. High-profile cases over which he has presided include the trial of Anthony Joseph, who stabbed Richard Whelan to death on a London bus after being confronted for throwing chips at Mr Whelan's girlfriend. He was also the trial judge for the case in which the former royal editor of the *News of the World* newspaper was jailed for trying to intercept voicemail messages left for royal aides of the British royal family.

Peter Wright QC, the prosecution barrister, was called to the Bar, Inner Temple, in 1981 and became a Queen's Counsel in 1999, and has served as a Recorder since 2001. The Chambers UK 2006 legal guide describes him as setting 'the benchmark for quality advocacy on the Northern Circuit' while *The Legal 500* 2007 cites him as a 'heavy-crime star'. This is a reference to his specialism in crime, particularly serious gang-related murder and drug dealing. His highest profile case was undoubtedly the successful prosecution of Dr Harold Shipman in 1999. Shipman was given fifteen life sentences for murdering fifteen of his patients in Manchester; in reality the death toll was probably in the hundreds.

Timothy Langdale QC, the defence barrister, was born in 1940 and was sixty-eight at the opening of the trial. Immensely experienced, he was called to the Bar, Lincoln's Inn, in 1966, and became a QC in 1992. He was a Recorder from 1996 to 1999. In a varied career, he was the Resident Assistant in the Community Justice Center, Watts, Los Angeles, from 1969 to 1970. He also acted as junior prosecuting counsel to the Crown from 1979 to 1987, and senior prosecuting counsel to the Crown from 1987 to 1992. His high-profile cases include the successful final appeal of the Birmingham Six, and the successful prosecution of child killer Roy Whiting for the kidnap and murder of eight-year-old Sarah Payne in 2001. Recently, he has acted more often as a defence counsel than as a prosecuting counsel.

The interior of Court 1 was shrouded in silence as everyone took up their places. Steve Wright was wearing the same suit as at his earlier appearances, and he looked bewildered as he sat wearing headphones behind a glass security panel in the dock. The hearing loop, earpieces worn hanging from Wright's ears with a small red box around his neck, was designed to amplify the voices of the barristers and the judge. At one point, Wright wrestled with the loop and tried to put it on his head before realising it was not meant to go there. Listening to the two leading barristers setting out a timetable for his trial, he heard it reaffirmed that his trial was expected to last between six and eight weeks, and that he denied all charges. It was obvious that no evidence would be heard on the opening day, and Wright spoke only to confirm his name.

The main focus of the first day was the selection of the jury, as in any trial of this size. The process is random selection from members of the public, but of course nobody serving on the jury can have any connection to anyone involved with the case. A pool of 114 potential jurors had to fill in questionnaires regarding any associations they might have with the five victims or their families, Steve Wright or his family, and their membership of certain occupations, including the media. The potential jurors were in another room, and Mr Justice Gross spoke to them via a video link. He directed them: 'The nature of this case is such that I must ask you to fill in a questionnaire that will be given to you as part of the process of jury selection. It goes to the heart of our system of justice... There are also in this case a number of reasons why it may be inappropriate for some of your number to sit on this jury.'

Eventually, the 114 were filtered down to twenty-four, twelve jurors being selected and another twelve held in reserve. The jury itself consisted of ten men and two women, a ratio that might seem strange, but theoretically there are no rules as to the gender composition of a jury – it is even possible to select an all-male or all-female jury, though uncommon. The jury was then sworn in, as it would be on each subsequent day of the trial. One of the male jurors would be taken ill during the early days of the trial, and would be replaced by a female reserve juror, making it a jury of nine men and three women.

The judge then directed members of the jury as to how they should conduct themselves. They should not attempt to do any of their own research, and they should ignore all media reports. He said: 'Do not try to obtain information elsewhere – for example, on the internet, about the case.'

That was the thrust of the opening day's activity, and the prosecution was expected to begin its case the following day.

Peter Wright QC duly spent 15 January giving a comprehensive introduction to the prosecution case, outlining the importance of the scientific evidence, witness testimony and CCTV footage to be used as key evidence. It was on the following day, Wednesday, 16 January, that the prosecution dropped its first series of bombshells in its evidence. With the daily proceedings making front pages and the main television news bulletins, these new facts and allegations electrified the media, as some of the secrets of the police inquiry and the scientific evidence began to be unravelled.

In court that day were members of the families of Tania Nicol and Gemma Adams. The father of Tania Nicol, Jim Duell, whom it will be remembered had found solace in religion since his daughter's murder, was accompanied by Tania's aunts Kipti, Finney and Donna Nicol, as well as Tania's half-sister Sarah Duell. Gemma Adams' father

Brian also sat in the public gallery, accompanied by a police family liaison officer. Wright's father Conrad and brother-in-law Keith Wright were in the media annex. They sat glum-faced throughout proceedings. Steve Wright's elder brother David sat in the public gallery.

Peter Wright QC referred to the Ipswich murders as a 'campaign of murder', and he said that the deaths of the five women 'were the work of the defendant, either alone or with the assistance of another'. It was said that a witness had seen more than one person in a car that was believed to have pulled up next to Tania Nicol a few minutes before she was last seen on 30 October.

Furthermore the results of the post-mortem on Anneli Alderton, found in woodland near Nacton on 10 December, posed questions about the feasibility of one person depositing her body. Peter Wright said that her body was 'deposited some distance from the road, yet there were no drag marks upon it'. He went on: 'In addition, there were no snag marks consistent with her naked form having been either dragged or carried through, past, under or over the low-lying branches and dense vegetation in the area. Of course, one possible explanation for this, we say, is that her naked body may have been carried by more than one individual.' Her body weighed almost 9 stone (57kg) and Peter Wright said that it was possible that her body was wrapped in something, or carried by someone with 'sufficient strength and stature to be able to carry her unaided to her final resting place'.

Peter Wright continued: 'If so, that individual would have needed to take sufficient care to have avoided her becoming entangled in low-lying branches or other vegetation. If this was done during the hours of darkness, it would take considerable effort and in all likelihood some form of illumination. If done during daylight, it would be at considerable risk of being seen, depending on the time of day.'

This idea of a possible accomplice would continue to hover in the air throughout the trial proceedings. However, there was no firm evidence of this, and the prosecution put its efforts into demonstrating Wright's guilt. Peter Wright said: 'Mr Wright was a user of prostitutes, a local resident of Ipswich, a man with transport and also the wherewithal not only to pick up prostitutes in the red light area of Ipswich, but also to transport and dispose of their bodies after killing them.'

Peter Wright QC also said that Wright had been stopped by the police the day before the discovery of the first body, that of Gemma Adams: 'In the small hours of December 1, his partner [Pamela] was at work. The defendant was again out cruising the red light district of Ipswich.'

It seems that the police had stopped Wright in his Ford Mondeo car and asked him why he was in the area. Peter Wright: 'His response was that he couldn't sleep and so he had gone out for a drive. In addition he gave the impression that he was unaware that the area of Ipswich in which he was driving was the red light district. This, we say, was palpably untrue. He lived locally and was a frequenter of prostitutes. His lie was not out of embarrassment; it was designed to conceal what his real motive was in being out that night. In the event you may conclude he elected not to continue his efforts to locate a suitable victim. He chose to return home and bide his time. It was only two days later that another woman (Anneli Alderton) went missing.'

It was confirmed that all five women had been asphyxiated, and they all had 'hyper-inflated lungs'. This suggested either drowning or strangling, the jury was told, although an exact cause of death had been established with only two of the victims. A shiver went through the court and the annexes when Peter Wright explained: 'The lungs of each of the women were hyper-inflated, consistent we say with them fighting for breath in the moments before their death.' He warned members of the jury that they would have to view distressing photographs of the women taken where they were found.

Peter Wright QC emphasised that the post-mortem examinations had been crucial in establishing links between the five deaths. It was confirmed that none of the women had suffered any other form of violence or sexual assault before they died, and they had no other significant injuries. Peter Wright then spoke about the women themselves: 'All were addicted to hard drugs such as heroin and cocaine, and were reduced at the time of their deaths to working the streets of Ipswich as prostitutes in order to survive.' It was ascertained that Paula Clennell had a high level of heroin in her blood, and that the other four women had also taken drugs.

The manner in which the five bodies had been found was also looked into. It was said that in at least four of the murders, the women were probably killed somewhere other than where their bodies were discovered. It was also concluded by a crime scene examiner that Anneli Alderton's clothes had been removed before she was deposited in woodland.

The jury was shown the crime scene photographs, but they were not displayed on the court monitor screen for obvious reasons. But Peter Wright went on to describe them verbally. He said that the exact positioning of Anneli Alderton's hair on the ground was very important.

But it was the revelation that two of the victims had been left posed in a cruciform position that raised collective eyebrows, and drew a gasp from some of those in the court. The two women left in this pose were Anneli Alderton and Annette Nicholls. The women were found lying on their backs with their arms outstretched at right angles to their bodies. In the case of Anneli Alderton, her left leg was slightly bent so that her knees touched, to form 'a classic cruciform shape', the jury heard. Very high quality computer graphics were used in court to show the position in which the two women had been found, to give the jury a better idea of the significance of this victim posing.

It should be remembered that the first two women found, Gemma Adams and Tania Nicol, were left in water. Peter Wright said that they had probably not drowned, and had been put there soon after being murdered. It was thought that Gemma Adams had been left nearer to Tania Nicol (who had disappeared more than a fortnight before Gemma), but that Tania's body had been swept southwards when the waterway flooded. Peter Wright said that Tania's body probably lay in Belstead Brook for five-and-a-half weeks before she was found at Copdock Mill. It was stated that Tania Nicol had a bruise on her arm and another on her knee that could have been caused by 'forcible restraint or manhandling'. Peter Wright also observed that Belstead Brook lies near the A14 road, along which Steve Wright used to drive to work on the Hadleigh Road industrial estate. After the body of Gemma Adams was found on 2 December, a new 'deposition site' was needed by the killer or killers, and the new site was also close to the A14 road.

Tania Nicol and Gemma Adams were not found posed in a cruciform shape, but then neither was Paula Clennell, who had been discovered close to where Annette Nicholls was found. Peter Wright QC said: 'Paula's body was not posed. It had all the signs of being hurriedly dumped.'

Peter Wright said that Steve Wright had the opportunity to carry out the murders when his partner Pamela was at work. It was stated that the murders stopped for a period when Pamela was off work because of sickness or annual leave. Peter Wright QC added that Steve Wright knew the area well, and as the prostitutes of Ipswich knew him, they felt at ease in his company when bodies started being found. He went on to say that CCTV footage of Wright's car on the nights that the girls went missing would be shown in court during the trial.

A witness had also seen a Ford Mondeo, the same as Steve Wright's car, in the Handford Road area of the red light district at the time that Tania Nicol was there on 30 October 2006, the night that she vanished. The court was also informed that Mr Wright's car was later seen by an automatic number plate recognition camera driving out of Ipswich, towards the area where the body of Tania Nicol was found. It was added that there was evidence to suggest that Wright's Ford Mondeo was again seen driving in the red light district on the night of 14/15 November 2006, when Gemma Adams went missing from the area.

Peter Wright QC said: 'The five women were systematically selected and murdered. There was a common denominator in each of their untimely deaths and that common denominator was the defendant, Steve Wright.'

After four hours of revealing and sometimes harrowing evidence, the court proceedings concluded for the day. The next day, Thursday, 17 January, saw the family of Paula Clennell in court, and proceedings were taken up largely by the DNA evidence against Wright. The fact that Steve Wright's DNA had been found on three of the victims – Anneli Alderton, Paula Clennell and Annette Nicholls, the three found on land – was looked into in detail. The fact that no DNA was found on Gemma Adams and Tania Nicol was not surprising, Peter Wright QC said, as they had been immersed in water for weeks before being found.

The jury was told that DNA had been found on the breast of Anneli Alderton, and that this matched the DNA profile of Steve Wright. Peter Wright QC said: 'The male profile matched that of the defendant. The probability of obtaining such a match by chance is in the order of one in a billion.' The fact that his DNA had also been taken from the bodies of Paula Clennell and Annette Nicholls lengthened these odds even further.

Peter Wright QC: 'The defendant must have had some form of close contact with each of these three women and that contact must have occurred shortly before their deaths.' He went on to allege that it was likely that the DNA would have been washed off by the women after the contact if they had been alive. He added: 'This contact cannot have occurred through random, coincidental and casual use of prostitutes. These findings point not to an unfortunate coincidence but rather to the defendant as being engaged in an active campaign of murder during the period from October to December 2006.'

The jury was informed that fibres had been found connecting Wright with more than one of the victims inside the footwell of his car, the sofa at 79 London Road, and on items of his clothing, including a jacket, lumberjack coat and three pairs of trousers. Light blood stains had also been found on clothing linked to two of the women.

It was also revealed that a pair of semen-stained gloves had been retrieved from Steve Wright's Ford Mondeo car. They contained DNA samples that could have come from Annette Nicholls and Anneli Alderton, the jury was informed. A forensic scientist was called by the prosecution, and concluded that there was 'very strong support' for the theory that Wright had been wearing them when he was in contact with Annette Nicholls and Anneli Alderton.

Peter Wright QC said that it would be 'highly unusual' for Wright to have worn the gloves when he was in contact with the two women if he was only engaging in consensual sexual activity. He said: 'Unless of course he was wearing the gloves having murdered the women and was about to dispose of their bodies.'

Steve Wright remained expressionless as all this was being said, but it was obvious that he was listening intently. He also occasionally looked at an evidence file in front of him that was several inches thick.

The defence team had to make some riposte to these allegations; Timothy Langdale QC said that he would challenge the significance of the DNA evidence. He also enlightened the jury as to Steve Wright's defence against the DNA evidence. This would feature later when the defence put forward its case, but Langdale realised the importance of responding at that point. He said that Steve Wright would not dispute that fibres and DNA linked to him were found on the bodies of the women. Langdale said that Wright was someone who used prostitutes in Ipswich and that he admitted having sex with four of the five women. The only one that he denied having sex with was Tania Nicol. He added that Steve Wright had picked up Tania Nicol, but had then changed his mind and dropped her off. Mr Langdale QC told the jury that it had to consider the world in which the women had operated, and the people associated with them. He said that the fact that Wright had had sex with some of the women explained the DNA link between him and some of the victims. Timothy Langdale: 'It's therefore not the case that the defence are suggesting some kind of freak coincidence. You have to consider the evidence, for example from the scientists, as to the real possibility of someone being able to kill the victims without leaving any trace on the body of the victims.'

Several journalists left the media annex to report this information when it was given.

By the close of that day, the direction to be taken by the defence team was coming into focus for the first time. On Monday, 21 January, the court reconvened, and after the jury was sworn in, it was taken out to view the 'deposition sites' as they were referred to in court. Jury members would also visit Wright's flat at 79 London Road and the red light district where the women had worked. They were driven in a coach surrounded by a convoy of five cars.

The following day, Tuesday, 22 January, the prosecution began to call its first witnesses. The jury was also shown

CCTV footage taken on the corner of Benezet Street in Ipswich's red light district, a known 'pick-up strip', as it was referred to in court. In the blurry image, recorded at around 11pm on 30 October 2006, a woman can be seen waiting on the side of the road; she had been identified by Kerry Nicol as her murdered daughter Tania. She had recognised her daughter by her cut-off jeans and pink-heeled shoes. Also on the footage at 11.01pm, 11.04pm and 11.07pm, a car alleged to have been Steve Wright's Ford Mondeo was recorded, prowling the red light district, said the prosecution.

Tania Nicol was the youngest of the Ipswich victims at just nineteen years of age, and the evidence of her mother, thirty-eight-year-old Kerry Nicol, in court that day reminded everybody, especially the jury, of the tragic human cost of the murders. Kerry Nicol told the court that she had 'no idea' that her daughter Tania was a prostitute. Her voice was full of emotion as she related how Tania had once been a bright schoolgirl, but she had had to face up to the truth that her daughter had led a double life.

Kerry said of her daughter: 'She said she had a job and was managing all right. She told me a few different things. She was a hairdresser at one point. Another time behind a bar in a pub.' But Kerry also told the court that she had answered a call from a massage parlour asking for 'Chantelle'. She had also found a note in Tania's room with that name on it, and men that Kerry did not know had called at the house. Kerry Nicol said that she thought her daughter was going out with friends at around 10.45pm on 30 October 2006, the night she disappeared. Kerry said: 'I was in the kitchen and I heard her go out of the front door. I heard the door slam.'

At 10.57pm, Kerry said that she had called her daughter to make sure that she had caught the bus safely, and that Tania had replied 'I'm fine.' Peter Wright QC asked Kerry Nicol if she had ever spoken to her daughter again. 'No,' replied Kerry, visibly shaking.

The court was told that three hours later Tania's mobile phone was not registering. The CCTV footage of Tania was all there was after the phone call, the court heard. Kerry Nicol explained that her daughter had left home at sixteen and started to take heroin. When she returned, her mother said, she was thin and her skin had deteriorated. Then living back at home, Tania had denied that she was still on drugs despite the fact that she had syringes in her room.

Kerry Nicol also told the court that she had received a series of phone calls from a stranger after Tania had disappeared. The man had given his name as Tom Stephens and he had asked if the girls would still go out to 'do what they do' if one of them was murdered. Kerry told the court: 'It was a strange thing to say.' Evidence was then given by a former policewoman, Alison Fenning, who said that she had later heard the same man talk to a prostitute about self-defence.

Also giving evidence that day was the mother of Gemma Adams, the second woman to go missing and the first to be found on 2 December 2006. Gail Adams told the court that she had not spoken to Gemma 'for months' and that the police had informed her that Gemma had gone missing on 15 November. Mrs Adams said: 'I had no idea how Gemma was living.' She had tried to call her daughter on her mobile phone, but could not get through.

The prosecution explained that Gail Adams had identified her daughter on CCTV footage taken on 14

November at 11.23pm in London Road, Ipswich. Then three more statements were given regarding Gemma Adams. A man known as 'Mr A' told the court that he had sometimes paid Gemma for sex after meeting her at a massage parlour in Ipswich. He said that he used to phone Gemma and meet for sex, and pay her sixty pounds. The last time that 'Mr A' had met Gemma was on 3 November. 'Mr A' said that she had been called by someone that she later described as 'Tania's sort of boyfriend' and that the conversation had been about Gemma going to the police about another girl who had gone missing. He had heard that Gemma had gone missing a short time later.

The second statement was made by 'Mr B'; he told the court that he would call Gemma on her mobile phone and meet her at a place of her choosing. He described Gemma as 'different, by far the nicest'. The last time he had met Gemma was on 10 November, five days before she disappeared, and they had full sex at an address on Blenheim Road (in the north-west of Ipswich town centre). He then added that five or six weeks earlier, Gemma had complained that a man had been giving her problems and would not leave her alone. The last statement was read to the court by Peter Wright QC. Given by Kim Grant, who used to go to school with Gemma Adams, it was related to a sighting of Gemma on Tuesday, 14 November.

Kim Grant had been a passenger in a car driven by her brother, and when they stopped at traffic lights at the Sainsbury's garage on London Road, Miss Grant had looked across and seen Gemma in the car next to them. Gemma had continued looking straight ahead and did not look around. When the lights changed, the car Gemma was in went on to Handford Road. Kim Grant said that she thought the car was dark in colour, but that she had been 'more interested in looking at Gemma'.

The next day saw a wide variety of evidence given. A witness called Jane Leighton told how she had seen Tania Nicol in the red light district on 30 October 2006, the night that she went missing. Miss Leighton said that as part of her weekly routine, she drove along Handford Road towards the town centre every Monday evening between 11pm and 11.20pm, and that on that particular Monday her attention had been attracted by a sex worker talking to somebody in a car. She later identified that woman as Tania Nicol.

Miss Leighton said that the car was shiny and navy blue, adding that it was a 'posh one' with a high boot. The witness admitted that she was not very familiar with car models, but that she had been able to select the vehicle model she had seen from a magazine that the police had given her. She said: 'There is usually someone along that road.'

Describing Tania Nicol, Miss Leighton said that she was 'very slim, quite tall, with long, straight hair hanging down', and that she was wearing a short denim skirt with no tights and a big puffer jacket. She also looked as if she was wearing boots. The woman identified as Tania was bent down with her hands on her knees talking to two men in the car, laughing and joking and shaking her head as she spoke to them. The fact that she had seen two men in the car was of course highly significant. She said that she could see that there were two men because the car's interior light was on. Miss Leighton told the court that she had not seen any other prostitutes on the road on that particular night.

Jane Leighton said that three weeks later she had been again driving along Handford Road on a Monday night, when she was stopped by the police who were making enquiries. She said that she had realised that the events they were asking about related to the night she had seen the woman talking to the two men in the car.

CCTV footage was also shown to the court of a dark blue Ford Mondeo car identical to Steve Wright's driving through the red light district. This use of visual props by the prosecution was very effective at driving its message home. But Timothy Langdale QC for the defence again said that Steve Wright was not involved in any way with the deaths of the five women, or indeed the disposal of their bodies.

Evidence was then given by a prostitute who had known all of the victims except Tania Nicol. Referred to as 'Miss D' in court, she described Anneli Alderton as 'cheeky, funny and quite loud'. 'Miss D' had worked as a prostitute for seven or eight years, and had worked in the Ipswich red light district in the autumn and winter of 2006. The jury was shown an electronic plan of the Ipswich red light area, and 'Miss D' said that she had also worked in an Ipswich massage parlour, Cleopatra's.

'Miss D' said that much of the street work was arranged by mobile phone, and that the girls usually met regular clients at prearranged locations. She had known Anneli Alderton for five or six years and she described their relationship as regular 'acquaintances'. 'Miss D' said that she took hard drugs, but she had never spoken to Anneli about whether she did too, although she had seen Anneli in the area of known drug spots.

She had seen Anneli, but she could not remember on

exactly which day. It was between 9pm and 11pm, and could have been a Sunday or a Thursday in December. Anneli had been standing at the junction of Handford Road and Burlington Road, looking at the cars going by. 'Miss D' had driven past on her way out of the town centre along Handford Road. In cross-examination, Timothy Langdale QC asked if Anneli had had a bag with her, but 'Miss D' could not remember. Langdale then asked her about a man called Tom Stephens, and 'Miss D' said that she recognised him, but that he had not been one of her clients. It was also said that Stephens often parked in a particular spot at Kingsley guest house in London Road, and that he was still parking there after the women went missing.

'Miss D' said that she had heard that Tom Stephens gave the women lifts from time to time.

Timothy Langdale QC then questioned her about other clients who may have given her some concern. Langdale asked if she remembered a client who drove a Vauxhall car and if he made her feel uncomfortable, and 'Miss D' replied 'Yes' to both questions, and told the court that the man had paid her for sex in locations around Ipswich.

'Miss D' also related how she regarded another client, who drove a 4 x 4, as 'strange'. He drove her to places as far away as Stowmarket and Sproughton. He was never violent, but once he had abandoned her when she got out of the car.

The boyfriend of Anneli Alderton gave evidence in the afternoon. A serving prisoner at the time of his court appearance, Sam Jefford told the court about the last time he saw Anneli. Jefford was living with Anneli in a flat in Colchester when she went missing. He said that he last saw her on the day she went missing, Sunday 3 December 2006.

They had had sex that morning, using no contraception, the court was informed. They got up at about 1.30pm, and he had walked her to the bus stop. He had expected to see her again that night. He said that Anneli did not have a mobile phone. He never saw her again.

The next day's proceedings, 24 January 2008, saw a witness being questioned about Tom Stephens. 'Miss F', a prostitute and also a friend of Paula Clennell, gave evidence from behind a screen. Saying that she had known Stephens since early 2006, she described him as 'cocky and arrogant'. She said: 'I always found him to be a bit weird and I didn't like him.' She said that she had spoken to Tom Stephens after he was stopped by the police on 16 December 2006. She said he was 'concerned about the way he had been treated' and that he thought the police were 'stupid' because they had not been aware that he had moved house.

Timothy Langdale QC for the defence read extracts from a police statement 'Miss F' had made, which made reference to Stephens driving all five of the women around.

'Miss F' told the jury that she found it strange that Stephens 'hung around' the red light district. She added that Stephens talked about Tania Nicol, saying that they had had sex in his bed. 'Miss F' said: 'I remember him saying that she shaved her legs in his bath.' She also said that he was 'worried' because he was afraid that DNA would be found on his sheets and in his bath.

There was also evidence given by witnesses regarding Paula Clennell, whose body had been found at Levington on 12 December 2006. One of the witnesses called, a taxi driver called Timothy Hoey, said that Paula regularly used his taxi service. On Sunday, 10 December 2006, the day that Paula went missing, he saw her on Burlington Road in Ipswich. He had pulled over about 15ft in front of Paula because the customer in his taxi wanted to wait to meet someone. After waiting for about three or four minutes he drove off. He said that he might have driven through the red light district again that day on his shift, but that he did not see Paula Clennell again.

Immediately afterwards, a 'Mr J' was called to the stand, hidden behind screens to conceal his identity. He said that after being paid at work on Friday, 8 December 2006, he took some hard drugs. He said that he did not know Paula Clennell 'very well' but that he had seen her at other people's houses, and that she used an alias on the streets, 'Kelly'. Two days later on 10 December he went into Ipswich to buy more drugs. He saw Paula near the junction of Norwich Road and London Road at about 4pm; Paula was also looking for drugs. 'Mr J' and Paula went to his car and they drove to a house in the Bramford Lane area (in the far north-west of Ipswich town centre and running northwards) and bought heroin and crack. They took the drugs together and then 'Mr J' dropped Paula off in the London Road and Handford Road area. He said that they had been together for about an hour, and that Paula still had some drugs left when he left her.

The court was informed that 'Mr J' also knew Annette Nicholls (whose body was found close to that of Paula very soon afterwards). 'Mr J' and Annette had been in a relationship together, and this had finished in October 2006.

The jury was then shown high quality 3-D moving graphics of the sites in Levington where Paula Clennell and Annette Nicholls had been found. As already revealed, Annette Nicholls had been posed in a cruciform shape, like Anneli Alderton, whereas Paula was on her front right side. Her hair had been caught in brambles. The court had already been told that it seemed as if she had been left in a hurry. A statement given by the man who found Paula Clennell's body was then read to the court. She was found at 3.02pm on 12 December 2006. A police helicopter discovered the body of Annette Nicholls nearby at 3.25pm. The jury was then told that it would be shown CCTV footage on the following Monday. The court was then adjourned for the weekend.

On Monday, 28 January the court viewed CCTV footage captured by cameras installed and run by the borough council and private companies, which the police had pored over minutely. Images of Tania Nicol in the red light district, Anneli Alderton on the train journey between Harwich and Manningtree (PC Craig Adamberry told the court that he thought Anneli took the train to Ipswich) and Gemma Adams in West End Road, Ipswich were seen. Timothy Langdale QC for the defence asked PC Adamberry if he was aware of Steve Wright and his car when he viewed the image thought to show Tania Nicol and a car identical to Steve Wright's Ford Mondeo. PC Adamberry accepted that he was aware of the defendant and his vehicle at that time, but that the police CCTV team worked away from the police incident room.

Peter Wright QC then told the court that the CCTV evidence would continue later, and that he wanted to turn the court's attention to Steve Wright's work record. Ian Fisher, an office manager for the Ipswich recruitment agency Staffbank, confirmed that Steve Wright had worked for the agency from August 2006 until his arrest, but that he could be contracted out to work for other companies. He added that before joining Staffbank, Steve Wright had worked for Gateway Recruitment in Nacton (based in Levington when he first started working for them) from February 2001 until he joined Staffbank, according to his records. He confirmed that Steve Wright had worked as a pub manager between 1989 and 1996.

During his time at Staffbank, Ian Fisher said, Steve Wright had worked as a forklift truck driver at Cellotex at Lady Lane industrial estate, Ipswich from 23 August 2006, and his shift had been between 8am and 4pm. From 30 November until his arrest he had worked at Cerro on the Hadleigh Road industrial estate. He said that Wright also worked some shifts at Felixstowe docks, loading and unloading, and that he was paid cash in hand for this. The focus of proceedings then turned to the work record and patterns of Steve Wright's common-law wife, Pamela. She had been working at the Ansaback call centre on the Ransomes industrial estate since August 2004. She worked the night shift from midnight until 9am on 31 October, 14 November, and 1–7 December 2006 inclusive, crucial dates for the case being tried, the court heard.

The prosecution then called the next witness, Ramon Delatorre, a handyman employed by a landlord owning properties in London Road. He had carried out work on the flat where Steve Wright lived with Pamela, the front flat at 79 London Road, and had worked regularly in the road at the end of 2006. He said that he would see Pamela Wright hanging out the washing at the back of the property, and on one occasion she had asked to borrow a tool to dismantle a bed. He saw Steve Wright cleaning his blue Ford Mondeo car once a week, and he would clean it 'inside and out'. He added that there was a CCTV camera attached to the side of 79 London Road, but that it was a 'dud' and contained no videotape.

The last witness before lunch was David Welton. He told the court that he lived in the same building as Steve Wright, in the flat opposite, and that his bedroom was 'wall to wall' with Steve Wright's bathroom. He said that he would hear Steve and Pamela Wright's washing machine being used after midnight 'two or three' times a week. He also told the court that on some occasions there would be 'a lot of thumping about' around midnight or one in the morning. He also said that Wright cleaned his car thoroughly 'most weekends'.

After the break for lunch, the proceedings returned to CCTV evidence. Andrew Wooler, a vehicle identification expert, told the court how he had tried to identify the make and model of a car seen on CCTV footage in connection with the case. The first images were taken on 30 October 2006, the night that Tania Nicol went missing, and were captured by a camera on Bibb Way, looking out onto Handford Road at around 11pm. He also viewed footage taken on the same night at the junction of Portman Road and Sir Alf Ramsey Way, close to the football ground. He had meticulously gone through many car makes and models and compared them with the images in order to find a 'unique feature' for positive identification. Mr Wooler said: 'In order to say categorically that the vehicle present on CCTV is a particular make and model, it is necessary to find a feature which is unique.'

Having looked at the possibility that the car in the images was a Volvo, a Nissan or a Saab, Mr Wooler said: 'I don't believe there's a feature that's 100% unique but that would be the only caveat that I would apply.' He went on: 'In my opinion it's highly likely that the suspect vehicle is a Mark III Ford Mondeo. From the work we've done we can't find another vehicle which matches the suspect vehicle as well.' He then identified the car seen in footage taken on 30 October 2006 at the junction of Portman Road and Sir Alf Ramsey Way, close to the football ground, and images looking down Portman Road towards Princes Street. In both cases he said that there was a 'high likelihood' that the car was a Mark III Ford Mondeo. Two features that were also taken into account between the CCTV images and Steve Wright's car was that the tax disc was placed higher on the front window than in most cars, and there was also a tree-shaped air freshener hanging from the rear-view mirror. Mr Wooler kept to the same line under cross-examination by the defence.

The court heard the next day a range of revealing evidence directed by the prosecution. Firstly, Alfred Smith, a resident of London Road, was called to the stand. He said that he had seen Steve Wright cleaning his car on two occasions. Mr Smith was working as a gardener in 2006. One morning Wright was cleaning his car at 7.30am. Mr Smith said: 'The bloke that owned the Mondeo was washing it down.' Wright had then hoovered the car, and the witness said that he had thought it was early in the morning to be hoovering a car. Next, Gordon Lawrence gave evidence. He lived next door to Steve and Pamela Wright, their properties separated by the access road or drive that leads to the car park at the rear. He said that he thought there was only one person living at No. 79, and that the person was a male. He said: 'As far as I knew there was only one person there. I only ever saw one person.'

The court then heard evidence about two occasions when Steve Wright was stopped in his car by the police during the Ipswich Police inquiry. PC Kerry Rumbellow said that motorists had been stopped on 2 November 2006 as part of random checks in relation to the disappearance of Tania Nicol three days earlier. Motorists were asked to fill in a short questionnaire. Steve Wright had been in his car with his 'co-habitee'. Asked whether he knew Tania Nicol, Wright had said 'No'. He had then been asked if he had seen anything unusual in the area since her disappearance, and if he had any information about prostitution activities in the red light area. To both questions he had also replied 'No'.

Almost exactly a month later on 1 December 2006 (the day before the first body was discovered, that of Gemma Adams), Steve Wright had been seen by the police driving slowly along London Road at 12.50am. The police officers concerned, PC Alisa Newman and PC Justin Wood, gave evidence in turn about pulling Steve Wright over. Firstly, a vehicle check had been carried out on the radio, establishing the owner as Steve Wright. The court was told that Wright was wearing a blue and red lumberjack coat with denim jeans. PC Wood said that Wright had a 'casual, slightly scruffy' appearance.

The rest of the details had already been presented to the court in the early days of prosecution evidence, with Wright saying that he could not sleep and that he was not aware that it was a red light area. PC Wood told the court: 'I gave him advice on the red light area, telling him that it was the red light area and the reasons why I stopped him...and if he was to be seen again by myself in the evening, I may report him for kerb-crawling.' A statement was then read by a statement clerk at Ipswich police station, confirming that Wright had presented himself there with his driving documents the next day.

A statement was then read to the court given by Andrew Ramsbottom, a police diver with Norfolk Constabulary. He had been a trained police diver for sixteen years, and on Friday, 8 December 2006 the diving unit had been deployed at the request of Suffolk Police. The divers were asked to carry out a 'wade search' of Belstead Brook, specifically in the area of Burstall Bridge. Mr Ramsbottom told the court that at the bridge the brook was relatively narrow, approximately 8ft (2.4m) wide. He said that in his opinion, the body of Tania Nicol, found some distance away at Copdock Mill, could have moved downstream from the area of the bridge. He said: 'It is my opinion that it is quite possible that a body placed in the river at Burstall Bridge could well have travelled the full distance' to Copdock Mill. He also told the court that in his opinion the body of Tania Nicol could have been put into the brook at Burstall Bridge.

The junior counsel for the prosecution, Simon Spence, then read a series of written admissions regarding Steve and Pamela Wright taking out a six-month contract on the flat at 79 London Road. He also stated that a car caught on CCTV footage taken on 30 October 2006 by cameras at Ipswich Town football club had been positively identified by the police as a Ford Mondeo.

Afterwards Peter Wright QC read out statements made by bosses at Steve Wright's last employers, Cellotex Ltd and Cerro. Dealing with minor employment details, they cleared up some points about the defendant's work record, including the fact that Steve Wright had never asked for any time off. Simon Spence then returned to read admissions to the court regarding the mobile phone records of Tania Nicol and Gemma Adams. He confirmed that no calls were received by Tania after 11.42pm on 30 October 2006. After that time, any calls were diverted to voicemail.

The court then heard a statement given by Paula Clennell to the police on 13 November 2006, in relation to the disappearance of Tania Nicol. It was chilling to hear her words that had been given so close to when she disappeared herself, and the court sat in tense silence.

In the statement, Paula said that her 'beat' was the Handford Road area of the red light district, while Tania Nicol worked more in the Burlington Road area. Paula said that Tania worked every night, and that sometimes they would share 'a cigarette and a chat'. Paula Clennell had said that she knew that Tania had worked for a year, and that she used the money to pay for crack and heroin. Paula had added that Tania was 'not the person to build up a drugs debt'. There was also reference made in Paula's statement to a man called Tom, who she said would collect Tania from home in his blue car and take her to work, and that Tania would pay Tom five pounds for petrol. She also said that she did not believe that Tania took the bus on the night she disappeared as had been thought. The statement read: 'This is not true – Tom would always collect her.'

Paula had said that the last time she saw Tania Nicol was between 12.30am and 1am on 31 October 2006. She said that Tania was collected in a silver car, perhaps an Audi or a Mercedes, and that the driver was white, had an average build, was in his forties, and had short dark hair. He did not have a beard, and was not wearing glasses.

Four days later, on 17 November 2006, Paula Clennell had given a second statement to the police. In it she had confirmed that the woman she had seen getting into the car was Tania Nicol, and that she had been asked to look at a copy of *Auto Trader* magazine in order to identify the model of the car.

Next, Sergeant Simon Hobson was called to the stand to explain how the police had viewed the CCTV footage during the inquiry. He explained to the court that a team of eight police officers and police staff had viewed about 10,000 hours of CCTV footage seized from 841 locations as part of the investigation, during a period lasting five months. The footage viewed was taken between December 2006 and late July 2007. Sergeant Hobson informed the court that the footage was graded into high, medium and low 'actions'. High actions were ones related to the suspect, and medium and low related to the victims.

Finally, the jury was told about the day of Steve Wright's arrest, 19 December 2006. The police had 'attended' 79 London Road at 4.45am. As they approached, they noticed that the light was on in the ground floor room. Steve Wright answered the door, and he was wearing a white polo shirt and a pair of blue tracksuit bottoms. The television was on, but was not displaying a picture. Detective Constable Butcher then arrested Wright on suspicion of murdering five women between 30 October and 12 December 2006.

Wright was cautioned, but he gave no reply. At that point he became unsteady on his feet and said: 'Let me sit down or I will fall down.' He was taken to Stowmarket police station, arriving there at 5.21am. During the journey, Wright was sweating and often had his eyes closed. Between 19 and 21 December, Steve Wright was questioned for eight hours and ten minutes. He had answered 'No comment' to all questions put to him. The court was then told of the detailed search made of his home. The police had seized his Ford Mondeo car, two pairs of work gloves, a jacket, a reflective jacket, a blue sofa and a pair of tracksuit bottoms. That was the end of the day's proceedings.

The following day was completely taken up by the evidence of the forensic pathologist, Dr Nat Carey. The main revelation heard by the court was that drowning could not be excluded as the cause of Tania Nicol's death. However, the evidence tended not to support that as the definitive cause of death, Dr Carey said.

A Home Office pathologist, Dr Carey had carried out the post-mortem on Tania Nicol at Ipswich Hospital on 9 December 2006, the day after her body was recovered from Belstead Brook at Copdock Mill. Dr Carey said that her body was decomposed from being in the water. She had last been seen on 30 October and the early hours of 31 October 2006.

Dr Nat Carey said: 'It was entirely consistent with her having died around or soon after the period of last sighting. The body must have entered the water within a few hours after the time of death, but I am not excluding the view that entry into the water was the cause of death.'

As with Gemma Adams' body, the lungs were hyper-inflated, and Dr Carey told the court that he had also found inhaled vomit in the respiratory system. He said that this was probably inhaled while she was still alive. This can happen when a person becomes unconscious or when asphyxia is involved, he explained.

Dr Carey said that there was bruising to the inner right upper arm of Tania Nicol, and a needle puncture mark near the elbow. There was also an injury to the back of her knee, which could have been caused by someone kneeling on it. There was also bleeding in the middle ears, which could be the result of drowning or asphyxia. But he stipulated that drowning could not be positively put forward; neither was it excluded.

Toxicology tests on the body had shown that Tania Nicol was 'significantly intoxicated' with morphine that had originated from heroin, the court heard. Dr Carey said that the presence of opiates in her body could have reduced certain indicators of the cause of death: 'I think it's entirely possible that she died with opiates in the body. The presence of the opiates may well have allowed other methods of death to operate without leaving obvious signs of violence.'

The next day, 1 February 2008, was largely taken up with DNA evidence. The court heard about DNA recovered from items belonging to Steve Wright and on the bodies of the murdered women. Dr Peter Hau, a forensic scientist with an expertise in DNA profiling, gave evidence first. Peter Wright QC asked him if internal DNA swabs taken from Anneli Alderton, Annette Nicholls and Paula Clennell contained any semen that could have come from Steve Wright. Dr Hau replied: 'No semen that could have come from Mr Wright was found on these swabs. The absence of semen on these swabs does not mean that sex did not take place between Steve Wright and these females, as it is possible to have sex without the deposition of semen in the vagina.'

Dr Hau confirmed for the jury that no semen was found

anywhere on the inside or outside of Steve Wright's Ford Mondeo car. The court then heard about a pair of gloves that was found inside a reflective jacket hanging in Steve Wright's hallway. They were found to be semen-stained. Low-level DNA that could have come from both Steve Wright and Paula Clennell were on the gloves. Again, the chances that the DNA could have come from anyone other than Paula Clennell were a billion to one, Dr Hau said. He added that it was likely that the semen was left on the glove when it was wet. Dr Hau said: 'There is very strong support for the view that Mr Wright was wearing the semen-stained gloves when in contact with Miss Clennell.'

Peter Wright QC then asked about the yellow reflective jacket itself. Dr Hau said that there was 'semen staining on the mid upper front and front of the left shoulder and on the back of the left shoulder'. Asked about blood staining, Dr Hau said that there were 'small amounts of light blood staining that, in my opinion, is contact blood staining'.

The semen on the jacket was tested for DNA, and it was found that there were components that could have 'originated from Mr Wright' as well as from Paula Clennell, said Dr Hau. The chances of it not being Paula Clennell were a billion to one again. With regard to the blood staining on the reflective jacket, Dr Hau said that it was also a billion to one chance that it did not come from Paula Clennell. On top of this, Dr Hau said that blood found on the lower right sleeve of the jacket could have come from Annette Nicholls. Again, the odds were a billion to one that it was not.

Dr Hau confirmed to the court that no DNA linked to

Tom Stephens had been found on the jacket, and that no DNA profiles other than that of Steve Wright, Paula Clennell and Annette Nicholls had been recovered from it. A lumberjack-style jacket that had also been taken from 79 London Road possibly had some semen staining on the right breast pocket, but this could not be confirmed, Dr Hau said. Two pairs of trousers and a pair of tracksuit bottoms taken from the defendant's home did not have either semen or blood on them, Dr Hau said.

Dr Hau was cross-examined at length by Timothy Langdale QC for the defence after the lunch break, largely regarding how the DNA could have been left on the items of clothing. Dr Hau also confirmed that there was low-level DNA on the body of Annette Nicholls from an unknown person. But the most significant exchange resulted from the evidence of seven tiny blood specks found in Steve Wright's car. Mr Langdale QC said that Dr Hau had made a statement two weeks earlier on 15 January that said that it was not normally possible to tell if DNA was left from blood specks or other bodily fluid. However, the DNA found in the blood specks had now been matched to the combination of Paula Clennell's DNA. This inconsistency was leapt upon by Mr Langdale QC, and he asked Dr Hau why he had changed his opinion.

Mr Langdale QC said: 'Forgive me, but you are a scientist and we know that it is your responsibility to produce accurate and reliable reports having thought the matter through carefully, and no doubt when you made your statement on 15 January you thought it through very carefully. What on earth made you add on the fact that you now say this result originated from the blood flecks?'

Dr Hau replied that he had changed his opinion when he revisited his conclusion. Mr Langdale QC asked him if he had communicated this change of opinion to anyone else. Dr Hau said that he had told Steve Wright's counsel the previous morning. He then confirmed that he did not make a further statement following his change of opinion. Mr Langdale QC said: 'This is not in accordance with normal practice is it?' Dr Hau said: 'No.'

But Dr Hau stayed firm in his belief that the DNA found in the car linked to Paula Clennell came from the blood flecks. He admitted that the car was not tested for saliva. Mr Langdale QC said: 'So you can't say what DNA traces were there in the Mondeo which were not from blood or semen.' Dr Hau said: 'No.'

Dr Hau also confirmed that although he had found a semen stain on one of the gloves that contained DNA that matched the profiles of Steve Wright, Annette Nicholls and Anneli Alderton, there were a further four DNA components that did not. Also, another semen stain on the gloves contained five components not in the DNA of Steve Wright, Annette Nicholls and Anneli Alderton.

The court was then adjourned for the weekend.

On Monday, 4 February, the court heard further DNA and fibre evidence. Dr Hau was still being cross-examined on the crucial DNA evidence by Timothy Langdale QC for the defence. The object of the exercise was of course to expose any weaknesses in the forensic evidence, the core of the prosecution case.

Steve Wright's reflective jacket and gloves were the main focus of the attack. The blood and semen stains on the reflective jacket had yielded some low-level (poor quality) DNA components, as already learnt. Mr Langdale QC wanted to know why further forensic tests were not carried out, to pinpoint the owner of that DNA, and whether it came from a person unknown to the police inquiry. Dr Hau repeated that there were signs of another contributor, but further tests would not have produced more definite results. Langdale persisted, and suggested that Dr Hau could not rule out DNA from 'unknown contributors'. Dr Hau said: 'Maybe, maybe not.'

Peter Wright QC stepped in for the prosecution and asked Dr Hau to confirm that semen was found on the reflective jacket, and Dr Hau confirmed this. He said that the results of the DNA components matching Steve Wright were the strongest, and that it was 'more likely' to have come from his semen. Dr Hau explained for the benefit of the jury that there was low-level DNA not from Steve Wright on the reflective jacket, but that this was not surprising because clothing often collects DNA from contact with other people.

The key point that Dr Hau made was that DNA matching both Paula Clennell and Steve Wright had been extracted from one stain on the jacket, and that this stain had no traces of low-level DNA components from other contributors.

Mr Langdale QC then questioned Dr Hau about the gloves, which had been found inside the pocket of the reflective jacket. Dr Hau told the court that there were a few possible cellular cells on the fingertips of one glove, but that no sperm heads were detected. Mr Langdale QC said that other stains on the gloves had given 'very weak and incomplete DNA profiles matching that of Mr Wright' and that two of the stains on the gloves had rendered no components that achieved the peak height required for routine reporting purposes. He then asked Dr Hau if he could determine whether the results came from a semen source or other cellular material. Mr Langdale QC: 'Bearing in mind that Mr Wright was the person who normally wore these gloves, it is not surprising to pick up his DNA from them.' Dr Hau agreed.

Mr Langdale asked Dr Hau about a stain found on the 'inner surface inside the thumb of the left glove'. He said that not only was there a low-level DNA mixture indicating Steve Wright and Paula Clennell, but there was also a further component that could point to a 'third contributor'. He asked Dr Hau why this was not investigated more.

Dr Hau: 'It hasn't been ignored, it has been considered. In this instance it was just so low level. In my opinion it was not scientifically worth doing.'

Peter Wright QC for the prosecution then questioned Dr Hau at length about his scientific methods for extracting DNA and determining its source, whether semen, blood, sweat or saliva. Although complex, it was useful for the jury to understand the process. Just before lunch, Peter Wright QC asked Dr Hau if sperm from any source other than Steve Wright had been found. Dr Hau said that no sperm from a third party had been detected aside from on one glove, where DNA from Steve Wright, Anneli Alderton, Anneli's boyfriend Sam Jefford (it must be remembered that they had had unprotected sex on the day of her disappearance), and a further person were present.

That afternoon, the court heard evidence from Ray Palmer, a forensic scientist with an expertise in fibres. Mr

Palmer explained that a fibre consists of individual components of thread that are very small and that the rate of fibre transfer depends on the duration and force of contact between two items. He added that most fibres were lost within hours of transfer, and that on very smooth surfaces (such as skin) which are exposed to the wind and rain, the rate of loss accelerates. He told the court that he had been asked to determine if there was any evidence of fibre transfer between any of the five women, Steve Wright and Tom Stephens. The extent of his evidence took some time to relate to the court and Ray Palmer informed the jury that he had identified a number of collectives of fibres that were 'of significance'.

Ray Palmer told the court that the tracksuit bottoms Steve Wright had been wearing when he was arrested contained fibres that matched those found on the naked body of Anneli Alderton. The eight blue polyester fibres had been transferred, and he had ascertained this by examining various 'tape lifts' that had been taken from her body. Mr Palmer also said that two fibres found on Anneli Alderton's body matched those found in Steve Wright's reflective jacket, and that seven 'variable grey' fibres and one pale brown polyester fibre matched another jacket found at Wright's home. There were also green-blue, red and purple-blue cotton fibres. These were linked to Wright's reflective jacket, but they were not 'constituent' fibres (part of the fabric), but matched the 'surface debris' on the jacket.

He told the court that he was aware that Anneli's body had been exposed to the elements for some time, and that the fibres he found would have been remnants of those deposited there.

The following day saw Ray Palmer continue to give his fibre evidence to the court. The revelation came that although Gemma Adams had been found in flowing water in Belstead Brook on 2 December 2006, fibres linked to Steve Wright had been found on her body. Mr Palmer said that there had been 'no expectation' of finding fibres on Gemma's skin as she was in water, but that fibres had been found in her hair. There was one red acrylic fibre and thirteen variable blue polyester fibres in her hair. These were left there by 'more forceful direct contact' and not by brief or casual contact, in his opinion.

Before examination, Gemma's hair had been washed because it had soil from the brook within it, the court was told. Ray Palmer said: 'We were looking for collectives of fibres which stood out that may have shown commonality with the other women.'

He added: 'In order for fibres to persist in such a hostile environment they would likely have been present in the deep linings of the hair itself, possibly tangled around the roots. In order for fibres to get into the deep linings of the hair there would have had to have been a fair degree of contact with the donor item in question.'

Peter Wright QC for the prosecution asked Ray Palmer: 'Did you find a match between the red acrylic fibre and various items from the defendant's home environment?'

Ray Palmer: 'Yes, we did.' He added that the red acrylic fibre in Gemma's hair corresponded with red acrylic fibres found on the bodies of Anneli Alderton and Paula Clennell. Also such fibres were found on the parcel shelf and rear seat of Steve Wright's Ford Mondeo car, the sofa in his flat, the tracksuit bottoms he was wearing when arrested and his checked coat. When Peter Wright QC asked if the red acrylic fibre found in Gemma's hair could have come from Belstead Brook itself, Mr Palmer said: 'No, in my opinion that explanation can be fairly reasonably excluded.' When asked if the thirteen other fibres could have come from the brook, Mr Palmer replied: 'I think we can eliminate the stream as being the source of the fibres.'

The court then heard that fibres had been found in the hair of Tania Nicol, also found in Belstead Brook a short distance away on 8 December 2006. Both Gemma and Tania had shoulder-length hair when they went missing, the court was informed. Mr Palmer explained that people with longer hair tend to have fewer fibres present in their hair, as they tend to run their fingers through it, and there is more chance of the hair being blown about by the wind.

Most importantly, a single black nylon fibre found in Tania's hair matched the carpet fibre in the passenger compartment of Steve Wright's Ford Mondeo car. Mr Palmer told the jury that nylon car carpets do not usually shed fibres easily as they are 'tough and durable'. After some more questioning from Peter Wright QC, Ray Palmer made his conclusion in regard to the fibre found in Tania Nicol's hair.

He thought that the fibres were transferred to Tania's hair a short time before her body was deposited in the brook. Ray Palmer said: 'In my opinion the findings provide moderately strong support for the view that Miss Nicol had been in forceful or prolonged contact with items which are or have been present in Wright's home environment around the time of her disappearance.'

It also emerged that many blue-yellow fibres were found on the surface of Steve Wright's tracksuit bottoms, and that these matched those found on the body of Annette Nicholls. Ray Palmer told the court that the red acrylic fibres found on Gemma Adams and Paula Clennell were also found on Annette's body.

In summary, the fibres found on Steve Wright's Ford Mondeo car, sofa and clothing linked him to all five dead women.

On the following day, 6 February, the case for the prosecution came to an end. The court heard that no fingerprints from any of the five women were found in Steve Wright's home or car. Simon Spence, junior counsel for the prosecution, said that fingerprints were found in forty-seven locations at the flat in 79 London Road, but they belonged to Steve and Pamela Wright and Pamela's son.

Simon Spence then read admissions evidence. A former colleague of Pamela said that she remembered Pamela trying to call Steve Wright three times on 10, 11 or 12 December 2006 at around 11pm. She had forgotten her glasses, but she was unable to get hold of Wright.

Next, it was said that a number of hairs were found in Steve Wright's Ford Mondeo car. Two of the hairs were said to match in colour and microscopic appearance the hair of Annette Nicholls. In the opinion of the forensic scientist who examined them, the findings provided strong support for the hair belonging to Annette. Mr Spence added that no hairs from the other four murdered women were found in the car. Following that, the toxicology reports were summed up. All five of the women had taken crack cocaine, cocaine or heroin in the hours before their deaths.

Details were then given regarding the questioning of

Steve Wright between 19 and 21 December 2006. These details had already been given earlier in the trial.

When the court adjourned for the day, the prosecution case was finished, and the defence case would begin to be put forward the following day.

On the morning of 7 February the court waited with anticipation for the opening of the defence case. However, not until the jury was informed at the last minute that morning did anybody realise what a remarkable few days they were to be: Steve Wright himself was going to give evidence in his own defence.

Timothy Langdale QC told members of the jury that he would not make a detailed opening statement, and he asked them to regard Steve Wright as 'any other witness', although there would naturally be a special focus on him. Langdale told the jury that Wright would explain how he came to live in Ipswich, how he came to use prostitutes, and how he met the victims in the case.

When Steve Wright approached the witness box, the atmosphere of the court was very tense, and there were gasps and one or two anguished cries from relatives of the murdered women. They were going to be sitting just feet away from the man accused of murdering a member of their family. Steve Wright was wearing his dark suit, white shirt and a pale blue tie. He looked tired and drawn, but he was composed in appearance. He was directed to the witness box by two security guards. He confirmed to the court that he was living at 79 London Road, Ipswich at the time of his arrest.

Timothy Langdale QC for the defence began by asking about the moment of Steve Wright's arrest (the court had earlier heard that Wright had asked to sit down when he was arrested). Steve Wright told the court that his reaction when arrested was due to feeling that he was going to faint. He said that a similar incident had happened a few years previously, when he was a prosecution witness in another trial. He had felt the same level of stress and passed out. He said that this could happen 'when I become under stress'.

Steve Wright then spoke about his background, as directed by Mr Langdale QC. Confirming that he was born in Norfolk, and that his father had been in the RAF, he said that he had attended schools in Malta and Singapore because of his father's job. His parents had divorced 'many years ago' and he had had very little contact with his mother since she left when he was young. His mother now lived in the United States, he said. His mother and father and grandparents had looked after him, he said. He told the court that he had a brother who lived in Bury St Edmunds and a sister who lived in Nacton, Suffolk. He had left school at sixteen with no qualifications and first worked at a hotel in Aldeburgh. At seventeen he joined the Merchant Navy, and then became a steward on the QE2 liner, where he met his first wife. They were married for about twelve years and had a child together. After leaving his job on the QE2, he had bought a bungalow in Halstead, Essex. He began to work in the pub business and he married again.

He told the court that he worked as a replacement pub manager before he and his wife took over the Ferry Boat Inn in Norwich in 1988. After that he worked as a pub manager in south-east London and Essex. He informed the court that he did not like it because of the drug scene. He said: 'Someone who's drunk you can figure out. Someone on drugs you can't so it becomes more dangerous.' Next Steve Wright said that he took over a pub in Haverhill, after which he moved in with his father in Felixstowe. At this time he admitted that he started to gamble on horses and got into debt. He told the court that he went to Thailand for ten weeks but when he came back his financial problems had got worse, so he eventually declared himself bankrupt. He registered with the Gateway Recruitment agency and stayed with it until 2006.

Timothy Langdale QC explained to the court that Wright did several different jobs while working for Gateway, the first one being at Supreme Foods in Hadleigh, Suffolk. Steve Wright confirmed that while he worked for Gateway, he visited its premises in Nacton twice a year. Mr Langdale then referred to a number of maps that showed the location of Gateway Recruitment and the deposition sites of the five bodies (Anneli Alderton had been found at Nacton, and Paula Clennell and Annette Nicholls just a mile (1.6km) south-east at Levington).

Mr Langdale asked Wright how he drove to Gateway, and Wright said that he used two different routes. One of them was the Nacton turn-off from the A14, and then along to the village. Langdale asked Wright if he ever drove along the road where Anneli Alderton's body was discovered. Wright said that he must have travelled on it 'numerous times' when he worked in Felixstowe, but not when he was working for Gateway.

Steve Wright went on to tell the court that he began using Ipswich massage parlours when he was living in

Felixstowe, but that he started to pick up prostitutes from the streets when he moved to Ipswich, as he thought that they would be cheaper. The massage parlours he had used were called Oasis and Cleopatra's, and he had used them about once every six months 'when he had the urge' while he lived in Felixstowe. He said that he tried to use different girls, and that he paid them between sixty-five and eighty pounds for their services.

Steve Wright said that he and his partner Pamela moved to 79 London Road from Bell Close on 1 October 2006, after Pamela had spotted the property. He told the court that he became aware of prostitutes working the streets in the area of London Road after 'a couple of weeks' of moving there. He began using the girls two or three days later, he said. The first woman he had picked up had been on Portman Road, close to the football ground. He added that he also became conscious of women working in Handford Road, West End Road and Sir Alf Ramsey Way. Wright told the court that he had not been aware that London Road was in the red light district until he was stopped in his car by the police in early December 2006. Wright said: 'I thought just Portman Road was the red light district.' He told the court that he would use prostitutes only when Pamela was at work and that he would pick them up and then go to a secluded spot with them.

Steve Wright admitted to the court that day that he had sex with Gemma Adams (last seen on 14 November 2006) in his car 'some time in the middle of November'. He also said that he had sex with Anneli Alderton in his flat on or around 3 December 2006, the day that Anneli was last seen catching a train. Wright added that he had decided not to have sex with Tania Nicol after stopping to talk to her because the acne on her face 'put me off'. He was asked if it was he who appears in CCTV footage taken at about 11.15pm on 30 October 2006, where Tania Nicol is seen talking to somebody in a dark blue car.

Timothy Langdale QC: 'Is that you picking up Tania Nicol on the corner of Handford Road and Burlington Road?'

Steve Wright: 'Quite possibly, yes.'

The court then heard how Tania had come to the passenger side window, spoken to Wright and then got into his car. Steve Wright: 'As she got into the car I noticed she had acne on her face and that is what put me off quite a bit really.' He told the court that he was driving towards Portman Road and at the same time trying to build up the courage to tell her that he did not want sex with her. Steve Wright: 'I drove further along Handford Road and turned into Portman Road and parked up. Basically I told her I had changed my mind.' He explained to the court that Tania had spent two or three minutes trying to get him to change his mind. Steve Wright: 'After she got out of the car I went home.' He said that she was in the car for 'probably about five minutes' and that he saw her walking back towards Handford Road.

Mr Langdale QC then asked Wright about the fibres found on Tania's body that were also found on his clothes and in his car and home. Langdale: 'Did you ever dispose of any items from your home environment because you thought they might connect you to those girls?' Wright said that he had not, and that his partner Pamela would have noticed if he had done so. When asked if he had anything to do with the disappearance of Tania Nicol, Steve Wright replied: 'No.'

Then Wright was questioned about pictures taken by a number plate recognition camera in London Road, showing his car travelling in the direction to go out of Ipswich at 1.39am on 31 October 2006. Langdale said that it had been suggested that he had been on his way to dispose of Tania's body. 'No way,' said Wright, going on to say that he had been unable to sleep. He said that when he was not able to sleep, he would often go for a drive along London Road, down the A14 to Nacton and then come back home through town.

Asked about another image, captured on 4 December 2006 at 1.49am (the day after Anneli Alderton was last seen), Wright said that he had again been unable to sleep. The court was informed that Steve Wright had picked up twelve prostitutes from the Ipswich streets, and had sex 'probably thirteen times' in this way in the three months before his arrest on 19 December 2006. When he was asked if he had ever picked up the same woman twice, he said that he had, and that he would drive around the red light district between 11pm and 2am looking for prostitutes.

Steve Wright told the court that he usually had sex with the women in his car, and when asked he said that there was never an occasion when they were completely undressed. He explained that he normally wore a pair of Tesco or Lotto tracksuit bottoms and his lumberjack coat when picking up the women. When pressed if he ever wore his reflective jacket at this time, he said that he did not, and that he wore that only to drive to work and back.

Steve Wright said that he always wore a condom when having sex with prostitutes, and that the women themselves would supply these. He added that he would use a pair of gloves to remove the condom after sex. Timothy Langdale QC: 'Why not use your hand?' Steve Wright: 'Because I found it distasteful.' Wright added that removing the condom with his bare hands would have made him 'gag' or feel sick. He went on to tell the court that he usually threw the condom out of his car window after sex, and put the glove he had used to take it off back into the side door pocket of the car. When he was asked if this was distasteful to him, Wright replied that it was not, as the glove would dry. The only time that he had ever got out of his car to throw away the condom was once after having sex with Gemma Adams, he told the court.

Next, Langdale asked Wright about the nature of the encounters with the prostitutes. Wright said that he would haggle with the women about how much he would pay for their services. They would want forty or fifty pounds, but he would pay twenty or thirty pounds. He added that there had never been any trouble with the women, and that they had never taken drugs while with him.

Timothy Langdale QC: 'Did you ever put pressure on any of the girls' necks?'

Steve Wright: 'Never.'

He went on to say that he was someone who sweated easily, especially when having sex. He explained that he would generally take the women back to where he had picked them up after having sex, and that the latest he would get home was about 2.30am. He said that he could survive on two or three hours of sleep a night. He also admitted to taking perhaps six women back to his home, but that he had only had sex with the prostitutes in the bed once. On the other occasions he had had sex with the women on the bedroom floor, because he did not want his partner (Pamela) to 'smell them'. The jury was then shown photographs of Steve Wright's bedroom, taken on the day of his arrest.

Wright told the court that when he took prostitutes back to 79 London Road he would drive to the back of the house and take them in through the back doors. When asked why he did this, he said that he did it to be 'secretive'. Wright added that he would lay his lumberjack coat and reflective jacket on the bedroom floor before having sex on top of them. When asked why he did this, he replied that he did not want to have sex on a 'dusty carpet'. He said that he used gloves in the house to dispose of the condoms also, and that these were kept in his coat pocket.

Steve Wright informed the court that the women were never allowed to go into the living room of the flat, as he was worried about them stealing. The women never objected to having sex on the floor, he said. Steve Wright: 'In the bedroom we would sit on the bed and basically discuss how much they wanted.' He added that the women were fully clothed at that time, but that he would ask them to be fully undressed during sex. 'They were quite willing,' he said. He then told the court that he and the prostitute would sometimes have a hug before she left.

Timothy Langdale QC then read out an admission that said the area around Wright's home was not under CCTV coverage. Wright confirmed that he was aware of a CCTV camera on the side of his house, about 12ft (3.65m) high up on the wall. He said that it was focused on the car park at the rear of 79 London Road. The court had previously been informed that this was a 'fake' camera. When asked if he was aware that it was a fake camera, Steve Wright said: 'No, I thought it just covered the car park at the back as it was a private car park.'

Steve Wright was asked if Tom Stephens was known to him. He said 'No.'

Timothy Langdale QC: 'Did you see pictures of a man called Tom Stephens who had been arrested by police?'

Steve Wright: 'No.'

Also during the day's proceedings it was revealed that Steve Wright had been convicted of theft in 2003. Wright had worked in the bar at the Brook Hotel, and he had been convicted of stealing eighty pounds. As a result, Steve Wright's DNA had been taken and put on the National DNA Database. This led to the match when DNA samples were taken from the deposition sites of some of the bodies of the dead women.

Simon Spence, junior prosecution counsel, added that Steve Wright had been placed under police surveillance on 18 December 2006, the day before his arrest. It also came out that Wright had lost his driving licence in May 2005 for speeding offences, and that he got it back in November 2005, when he bought his Ford Mondeo.

On 12 February, Steve Wright continued to give evidence from the witness box, but this time he was being cross-examined by Peter Wright QC for the prosecution. In court that day, Steve Wright repeatedly denied that the fibres found that linked him to the five dead women proved that he was involved in their deaths or the disposal of their bodies.

Firstly, Peter Wright QC questioned the defendant about the blue fibres found on the body of Tania Nicol. Steve Wright repeated his earlier evidence that Tania had been in his car for only a short time, and that there had been no contact between them. He said that he could not say how the fibres came to be in her hair. Peter Wright QC then asked him if it was another coincidence that fibres had been found on the bodies of Anneli Alderton, Paula Clennell and Annette Nicholls. Steve Wright said: 'If you say so, yes.'

Steve Wright told the court that there was no possible reason for Tania Nicol's head to come into contact with the carpet in his car. Peter Wright QC: 'Not unless that happened while you were killing her. Or carrying her body in the back of your car.' Steve Wright denied this.

Peter Wright QC next asked how blue fibres had come to be on Steve Wright's reflective jacket and Steve Wright said that he could not say. Peter Wright QC: 'Whilst you were disposing of her body you were wearing your reflective jacket and there was a cross-transference of fibres from your clothing into her hair. Or while you were squeezing the life out of her?' Steve Wright denied this also.

Attention was next turned to the variable blue polyester fibres found in the hair of Gemma Adams. Asked if this was another coincidence, Steve Wright said that he could not say.

Peter Wright QC: 'It would appear, therefore, that in the hair washings of these two women, both of whom were deposited in water in or near Belstead Brook, that they both had variable blue polyester fibres found matching two items of your clothing. Is that another coincidence?'

Steve Wright: 'I couldn't say.'

Asked about the red acrylic fibres taken from the back of his car, Steve Wright said that he did not know how they got there, saying that he did not own an item like that and that he had not disposed of an item like that.

Steve Wright: 'Red acrylic means nothing to me. I have no idea where they came from.'

Peter Wright QC: 'They came from the blanket in which you carried some of the bodies. That's where they came from, didn't they?'

Steve Wright: 'No.'

Turning to the red acrylic fibres found on Anneli Alderton's body and on the hair tape lifts (tapes used to extract foreign fibres and substances from hair), Peter Wright QC asked if this was also a coincidence. Steve Wright: 'I couldn't say.' Peter Wright QC continued asking questions about Anneli Alderton.

Peter Wright QC: 'She also had your DNA on her right breast, didn't she?'

Steve Wright: 'If you say so, yes.' Peter Wright QC: 'Did you carry her from the road at Nacton through the woodland to her resting place?' Steve Wright: 'No, I did not.' Peter Wright QC: 'Did you carry her in a blanket in order to disguise or conceal what you were doing?' Steve Wright: 'No, I did not.'

Peter Wright QC: 'We know from the evidence in the case there were no drag or snag marks on her body. That I suggest was because she was covered in something. Is that right?'

Steve Wright: 'I couldn't say.'

Peter Wright QC: 'We know from the scene that Anneli Alderton was found in that there was a considerable amount of low-lying vegetation. Yet she had no drag marks or scratch marks on her body. Did you strip her at the scene?'

Steve Wright: 'No, I did not.'

Peter Wright QC: 'Is that when your eleven blue-grey polyester microfibres were shed on to her body?'

Steve Wright: 'I couldn't say.'

Peter Wright QC then turned the attention of the court to the early hours of 4 December 2006, when Steve Wright's car with a man inside wearing a fluorescent jacket was captured by an automatic number plate recognition camera. Asked if he was driving with Anneli Alderton's body in the car in the image, Steve Wright denied it.

Peter Wright QC: 'Were you driving out to find a different venue?'

Steve Wright: 'No, I did not.'

Peter Wright QC: 'The reason why your fluorescent jacket fibres are on her body is that you dumped her there.'

Steve Wright: 'No, I did not.'

Peter Wright QC then said that there was a link between the way that the bodies of Anneli Alderton and Annette Nicholls were posed (in a cruciform shape), between the places where they were deposited, and between the fibres found on their bodies. Every time Steve Wright said, 'I couldn't say.' Peter Wright QC went on to ask how Steve Wright's DNA had got on to Annette Nicholls' body in several places, and about the semen stains found on Steve Wright's gloves.

Peter Wright QC: 'Is that because, having killed her, you put on your gloves and disposed of her body?' Steve Wright: 'No, I did not.' The prosecutor then referred to a scratch that was present on the cheek of Annette Nicholls, and the fact that blood matching that of Annette was found on Steve Wright's reflective jacket. Peter Wright QC: 'Is the reason why her blood is on your jacket that you carried her dead to where she was deposited, and in carrying her there she scratched her face on the brambles and low-lying vegetation?'

Steve Wright: 'No, I did not.'

When Peter Wright QC asked how Paula Clennell's blood was found on the reflective jacket, Steve Wright said that he had 'no idea' how it could have got there. Peter Wright QC: 'The blood got there when you were dumping her body.' Steve Wright: 'No, it did not.'

When asked, Steve Wright admitted that it was possible that his Ford Mondeo car was parked on the Old Felixstowe Road close to Levington on 8 December 2006 at around 8.30pm.

Peter Wright QC: 'Was that you looking for a suitable place to dump your next victim?'

Steve Wright: 'No, it was not.' The prosecutor then said that the body of Annette Nicholls was left near that road later that night.

Referring to the blood flecks linked to Paula Clennell found on the back seat of Steve Wright's Ford Mondeo car, Peter Wright QC asked how they got there. Steve Wright replied that he did not know how they had got there, and that Paula had not sat on the back seat.

Peter Wright QC: 'Did you kill Paula Clennell during a similar sexual encounter?'

Steve Wright: 'I did not.'

Peter Wright QC: 'Did you then put on your gloves, leaving a deposit of semen on the inside thumb?'

Steve Wright: 'I did not, no.'

Peter Wright QC: 'Did you then dispose of her body wearing the gloves and reflective jacket?'

Steve Wright: 'I did not, no.' Finally, Steve Wright was asked how his DNA came to be on Paula Clennell's body. He said that he did not know why this had happened.

Also that day in court, the prosecution turned the

spotlight onto Steve Wright's Ford Mondeo. Peter Wright QC focused on the state of the car when Steve Wright was arrested on 19 December 2006. Steve Wright had previously said that he took pride in the car and that he cleaned it regularly. However, when it was seized, it had cigarette ends from his partner Pamela's son inside, as well as a Mars bar wrapper in a front door pocket. Peter Wright QC: 'Is that the position you had reached with this, Mr Wright. So successful had you been at picking up these women and killing them that you were getting sloppy.' Steve Wright: 'No way. I had nothing to do with their deaths.' Peter Wright QC then asked if Steve Wright only cleaned his car when he had a reason to do so. Steve Wright: 'No, it was cleaned regularly.'

Asked if he remembered ever cleaning his car in the dark, Steve Wright said that he could not remember doing so. Peter Wright QC: 'Well, that would be an odd thing to do, wouldn't it?' Steve Wright: 'It would, yes.'

Steve Wright was then shown photos of his Ford Mondeo car taken on the day of his arrest, and he agreed that it did not look particularly clean. Peter Wright QC: 'It doesn't appear to be the case that this interior had been cleaned for some time.' Steve Wright agreed, and said that he had not cleaned it for 'a few days'.

When questioned about the last time he had been in the company of his partner Pamela's son, Steve Wright said that he could not remember. Peter Wright QC asked Steve Wright if Pamela's son Jamie last visited them days, weeks or months before the arrest.

Steve Wright: 'I really can't say.'

Peter Wright QC: 'I can't remember? We know that when you were arrested your vehicle was searched. That's right, isn't it?'

Steve Wright: 'Yes.'

Peter Wright QC: 'And we know that in your vehicle there were some cigarette ends. That is correct, isn't it?'

Steve Wright: 'If you say so, yes.' The prosecutor then said that a DNA profile that matched Pamela's son Jamie was taken from the cigarette ends. He asked if Jamie travelled in the car. Steve Wright: 'He has done on occasions, yes.'

Peter Wright QC: 'So is it possible to cast your mind back as to the last time he was in your company in the car?'

Steve Wright: 'I can't, no.'

The prosecutor then asked if Jamie had visited Steve Wright and Pamela in November 2006, when Pamela was off work sick for a period of time. Steve Wright: 'I can't remember.'

Moving on to the semen-stained gloves found in the car which Steve Wright had said he used to remove condoms after sex with prostitutes, Peter Wright QC said: 'The reason you used those items was that you felt repulsed by the bodily fluid that may be on the exterior.' Steve Wright: 'I did, yes.' Peter Wright QC: 'That's a nonsense, isn't it? It's a feeble attempt to explain away the presence of semen staining on the inside and outside of those gloves, isn't it?' Steve Wright denied that. Asked why semen stains had been found on both the inside and outside of the gloves, Steve Wright said: 'Sometimes when I leave work I pull the gloves off by the wrist band and they turn inside out.'

Peter Wright QC asked if it was a coincidence that neither pair of gloves, found in the car and the pocket of the reflective jacket hanging in the hallway, had been found inside out. Steve Wright said that he could not say.

Questioned why he did not use wipes to remove condoms instead of the gloves, Steve Wright replied that it was because he did not have any in his car. Steve Wright was then shown some items that had been found in his car, and amongst them was a packet of wipes used to clean a car windscreen. Steve Wright told the court that he did not use the wipes because he was afraid that there might be 'chemicals' on them.

Peter Wright QC: 'You were prepared to use the gloves that you use during the course of your work in order to take off the condom on your penis. Were you not concerned that they might have chemicals on?'

Steve Wright: 'No, I wasn't.'

At the end of the cross-examination, the court heard that after his arrest, Steve Wright had refused to answer any questions put to him by the police on the advice of his solicitor. The prosecution alleged that Steve Wright would have given answers to these questions if he had already worked out his story, the one given in court.

Peter Wright QC: 'Or was it that you were quite simply happy to sit behind the advice that you were then being given because the truth was you had absolutely no explanation to give? You had not then come up with this account, seeking to tailor it to fit the forensic evidence in this case.' Steve Wright denied this.

Peter Wright QC: 'In so far as your account is concerned it's an act of desperation on your part to try and explain away those suspicions between you and the murder of each of these women.'

Steve Wright: 'No, it was not.' Peter Wright QC asked him why he had not given these explanations to the police officers after his arrest. Steve Wright: 'By that time I was in such a state that I couldn't think straight, I couldn't think of anything at the time.'

Peter Wright QC (in conclusion): 'The sad truth is, Mr Wright, you engaged in a campaign of murder for a little over six weeks. That's the truth. Selecting women with which to have sex with and kill.' Steve Wright denied this.

Steve Wright was then examined again by his defence counsel, Timothy Langdale QC. Langdale asked him about the times that he went out for a drive when he could not sleep and what he did. Steve Wright told the court that he would go to Felixstowe sometimes, and walk along the promenade there for fifteen minutes and have a cigarette. When asked, he said that it was possible that he wore his reflective jacket on these occasions. Other times he would not go as far as Felixstowe, and he would stay in his car. That was the end of Steve Wright's evidence, and the court felt drained by the end of it.

There was also evidence heard that day regarding Tom Stephens, the first man to be arrested in Trimley. Defence counsel for Steve Wright read out written statements to the court. The first came from a Miss L, who said that she had had an affair with Tom Stephens in 2004. She said that she had met Stephens through a lonely-hearts column in a newspaper. She said that they had met for sex five times, and at this time he was 'never scary' and always 'polite'. One time, Tom Stephens had wanted to hold her down during sex, and he had suggested that they use 'a safe word' so that he would know when to release her. Miss L said that she had refused to do this, but that on a couple of occasions he had overpowered her and this had made her feel uncomfortable. She said that Stephens had pinned her down with his hands on her shoulders and across her neck.

Miss L said that she had borrowed five hundred pounds from Stephens to pay a council tax debt. She said that Stephens had described this as 'a friendly loan'. In late August 2004 she decided to end the relationship, and Stephens had offered to waive repayment of the loan if she slept with him one more time.

The court heard that Miss L moved in with a friend, Miss M, in February 2005. Miss M said in her statement that Stephens had made several calls to their address and told her that he was 'pursuing a debt and had stalker's rights'. At Easter 2005, Stephens had driven across the country to Miss M's home to see Miss L. In April 2005 he told Miss M that he was 'going to kill both women'. Miss L had reported this to the police, and she had changed telephone numbers, she said in her statement. Tom Stephens was given a harassment order, and the two women had not seen him since the summer of 2005.

With that, the court adjourned for the day.

On 14 February Peter Wright QC began his closing speech for the prosecution, summing up the case for the Crown against Steve Wright. For the benefit of the jury, he broke it down into five key issues that they needed to consider in reaching their decisions. He explained to them that they had now heard all of the evidence and that it was now their responsibility to reach verdicts. As seen, the evidence in the trial had been complex and the prosecution was keen to make sure that the jury did not get mired in too much detail.

Peter Wright QC: 'Let us start by considering the most

important document in the entire case – the indictment. It's the document which you will be invited to return verdicts upon.'

The indictment stated five counts of murder: 'On a day between October 29 2006 and December 9 2006 the defendant murdered 19-year-old Tania Nicol. On a day between November 13 2006 and December 3 2006 he murdered 25-year-old Gemma Adams. On a day between December 2 2006 and December 11 2006 he murdered pregnant 24-year-old Anneli Alderton. On a day between December 7 2006 and December 13 2006 he murdered 29-year-old Annette Nicholls. On a day between December 9 2006 and December 13 2006 he murdered 24-year-old Paula Clennell.'

The five key issues for the jury to consider were as follows:

1 Were the deaths of the five women murder or misadventure?
2 If they were murders, were they connected?
3 Was one person involved, or another, or others?
4 If there was more than one person involved, were they operating together or independently?
5 Was the defendant responsible in respect of each of the five counts?

Peter Wright QC went on to remind the jury of the common links between the five women. He said that they were all addicted to drugs, they turned to prostitution to fund their habits, and they all met the defendant on the night of their deaths. He added that all five women took drugs leading up to the time of their deaths, but that this was not the sole reason for their deaths, it was just a 'fact of their lives'. He told the jury that there were high levels of morphine found in the bodies of all five women, but that this was only significant in terms of their vulnerability. The degree of their intoxication would have depended on their tolerance to drugs, he said, and then reminded them that it was the prosecution's case that the women 'died with drugs on board' rather than as the result of an overdose.

All of the five women were sex workers in Ipswich, slim, relatively young with long or shoulder-length hair, he informed the jury, and they all died within six-and-a-half weeks of each other in unusual circumstances. He went on to say that all five women had suffered either hyper-inflation of the lungs, or injuries consistent and corresponding with compression of the neck. In all five women, death was consistent with asphyxiation or an interference with 'the normal mechanics of breathing'.

Peter Wright QC told the jury that none of the women had suffered significant injuries before their deaths and none of them had a pre-existing condition that could have caused death. All of their bodies were found naked in rural or semi-rural areas, he added.

Peter Wright QC: 'We say these deaths were not unconnected and unrelated incidents of misadventure. They were linked and entirely deliberate.' He added that when the evidence was viewed as a whole, it suggested murder by 'a man or men'. Referring to the fibre evidence that linked Steve Wright to the victims, the prosecutor said: 'The coincidences are multiple. This was not misadventure. This was murder and part of a pattern. It started with the disappearance of Tania Nicol and concluded with the death of Paula Clennell.'

Next the prosecution turned to the unresolved idea that the murders could have been committed by more than one person. Peter Wright QC: 'You have heard a lot of evidence throughout this case in terms of the possibility that this may have been a series of offences committed by a man or men and you have also had brought to your consideration a particular individual called Tom Stephens.' He went on to say that it may never be known if another person was involved: 'We cannot exclude the possibility that another or others may have had a hand in each of these deaths.' He added that this was 'complete speculation', however.

Peter Wright QC told the jury that the 'spectre' of Tom Stephens had been raised by the defence and that the prosecution had to deal with it. He followed this by saying that Stephens did act suspiciously and irregularly during the period in question. He said that Stephens had links with all five women, made 'unusual and disturbing' remarks, regularly went to the red light district and also frequently visited the police unit that had been set up in that area.

Peter Wright QC continued to refer to Tom Stephens: 'But in terms of evidence of wrongdoing on his part and his possible involvement in these matters it is merely a matter of conjecture. A lack of evidence proving innocence cannot be created into evidence proving guilt – however skilfully it's presented.' He reminded the jury that although Stephens had been arrested, his home and car searched, his DNA taken, and interviewed by the police, he was never charged with any offence. Peter Wright QC: 'His role is not central to the issues in this case.'

The prosecutor went on to say that even if more than one person had been involved, the chances that they acted independently of one another were so slim that they could be discounted. He said that Steve Wright was the common denominator in the murder and disappearance of the women. He added that the chances of Steve Wright only being involved in the disposal of the bodies was so unlikely that it could also be dismissed.

Referring to Steve Wright, the prosecutor said: 'That's not what happened here. He was the killer.'

Peter Wright QC also repeatedly asked the jury about the series of 'coincidences' in Steve Wright's links with the five dead women. Going through key evidence points, including blood, DNA, fibre and CCTV evidence. At the end of each point, he made the remark 'Singular misfortune or significant fact?' again and again. The effect was dramatic, and the court was gripped as he built to a crescendo.

Peter Wright QC said: 'The sad fact is – and for reasons only known to himself – as we said at the outset of this case, Steve Wright embarked on a deadly campaign in late 2006 that ended in the murder of these five women, of which he is guilty.'

That concluded the closing speech for the prosecution.

The following day, 15 February, saw the closing speech for the defence, delivered by Timothy Langdale QC. Addressing the jury, the skeleton of the defence case was that the killings involved a greater degree of planning and skill than Steve Wright was capable of. Tom Stephens was brought into the equation and Steve Wright's behaviour was not that of a murderer, it was claimed. Also, Mr Langdale questioned the prosecution evidence at length.

Timothy Langdale QC questioned the fact that none of the clothing of the women had been found, despite a huge and intensive police search. Mr Langdale: 'What on earth is it about Steve Wright that enables him, as a pretty ordinary sort of bloke, to dispose of the clothing of all of these women without leaving a trace? At the same time the man who is so 'sloppy' leaves blood on his reflective jacket and does not even bother to take that off. How does that square with common sense?'

Timothy Langdale QC asked the jury why Steve Wright would wear a reflective coat to dump a body. He said that it made 'no sense at all', and asked the jury what more a man could do to draw attention to himself (than wear a bright yellow reflective jacket). He also said that Steve Wright did not know very well the areas of countryside where the five bodies were deposited. Continuing, he pointed out to the jury that there was no evidence that Steve Wright went for walks in the countryside, and that hundreds or thousands of people around Ipswich may know the area being considered. Langdale reminded the court that Tom Stephens, who was arrested but not charged, knew the stretch of road to Nacton where Anneli Alderton's body was dumped.

The defence then questioned the idea that all of the bodies were disposed of by the same person or persons. Timothy Langdale QC said that whoever disposed of the bodies of the last three women – Anneli Alderton, Annette Nicholls and Paula Clennell – was almost attempting to draw attention to the way that they were left by making no attempt to conceal them. He told members of the jury that they must ask themselves what conclusions they can draw from the prosecution case, and whether it was the same person or people responsible for the deaths of the victims. Mr Langdale QC: 'It may well be that it was not the same person. Quite clearly you may think that the bodies of Tania Nicol and Gemma Adams were deliberately placed into the water of Belstead Brook. No doubt you will conclude that was done for a reason that the person or people who did it had something specific in mind.' He added that the reason was to prevent the bodies being found for 'as long as possible' and to wash away evidence.

Mr Langdale QC went on to say that the bodies of Anneli Alderton, Annette Nicholls and Paula Clennell were found in 'very different locations' and posed in what had been termed 'a trademark way'. He added that the prosecution claimed that Paula Clennell did not end up in the cruciform pose because 'the person responsible was disturbed in some way'. The defence suggested that this evidence showed inconsistencies between the first two victims and the last three. Mr Langdale QC told the jury: 'The prosecution allege it is the same killer, or killers, and allege the discovery of Gemma Adams' body caused him to change the locations of the bodies. You will have to consider that evidence.'

The defence then moved on to the fibre evidence presented by the prosecution witness Ray Palmer. Mr Langdale said that it was important that the prosecution could not rule out that the carpet fibre evidence found in the hair of Tania Nicol (linked to Steve Wright's Ford Mondeo car carpet) could have come from the back seat of the car. Mr Langdale: 'It is perhaps very important Mr Palmer cannot rule out the possibility that the fibre came from another car altogether. These girls were hardly strangers to the interiors of other people's cars and it is not as if Wright's car was some special breed of car with special material. God knows how many would be using the same carpet.'

Timothy Langdale QC told the jury that the prosecution claim that for the fibre to get into Tania's hair would take 'forceful contact' seemed to him to be no more than speculation. He asked the jury why Steve Wright would tell them that Tania Nicol was in his car hours before she disappeared if he was 'tailoring' his evidence to fit the scientific evidence heard in the trial. Langdale also asked why Steve Wright would not just say that he had sex with Tania in the back of his car, instead of explaining that he was with her for five minutes before making her get out of his car.

Mr Langdale QC then referred to the CCTV footage taken at 1.39am, 1 November 2006, showing Steve Wright's Ford Mondeo heading out of Ipswich. He said that if Steve Wright was driving to dispose of the body of Tania Nicol, the camera seemed to have 'missed him coming back'. Mr Langdale continued: 'It seems also to have missed him taking Gemma Adams' body out on 15 November – that is another thing the prosecution suggest.'

Returning to Tania Nicol, Mr Langdale said: 'It is the prosecution's case that Tania Nicol was murdered not long after she got into Wright's car at around 11pm on October 30 (2006). What is he doing waiting till 1.30am in the morning to drive her body out of town? What is taking all the time?' He told the jury that if Steve Wright had been responsible for Tania's murder, then he would have wanted to get her out of Ipswich as quickly as possible.

Staying with Tania Nicol, Timothy Langdale QC told the jury that there was evidence to suggest that she was still alive after she left Steve Wright's car. Steve Wright had already told the court that Tania got into his car at 11.09pm on 30 October 2006, and that she got out again five minutes later. Mr Langdale quoted witness evidence from Jane Leighton, Kerry Land and Helen Brooks. Jane Leighton had said that she had seen a woman she thought to be Tania Nicol talking to men in a 'posh' car between 11pm and 11.20pm on that night. Mr Langdale QC: 'Is it possible that Jane Leighton saw her (Tania) at 11.20pm after that encounter, having got out of that car? It cannot be dismissed.'

Kerry Land, a worker in the nearby Sainsbury's petrol station, said that she had seen Tania at 11.45pm that night, but in different clothing; she was 85 per cent sure that it was Tania Nicol. Helen Brooks, a Royal Mail worker, said that she had seen somebody she thought to be Tania talking on a mobile phone at 3.45am on 31 October 2006.

Finally, Mr Langdale told the court that Paula Clennell herself had said in a statement to the police that she had seen Tania Nicol on 31 October 2006 between 12.30am and 1am. Mr Langdale QC: 'Steve Wright did not kill Tania Nicol, someone else did after she left his car.' He told members of the jury that they must ask themselves if they agreed with the evidence that Tania Nicol was seen again later that night.

Focusing on Gemma Adams, Mr Langdale said that it could not be ruled out that the fibre evidence found in her hair was left there when she had sex with Steve Wright. He told the court that Ray Palmer's fibre evidence had seemed overwhelming until he was cross-examined. Mr Langdale said that it had come as a 'bolt from the blue' when Mr Palmer had admitted when questioned that Gemma had 'at least 216 other fibres in her hair'. Mr Langdale QC: 'What a pity those were not mentioned by Mr Palmer.'

Making his closing speech for the defence to the jury, Timothy Langdale QC said that there was a reasonable possibility that someone other than Steve Wright had committed the murders. He said that the fibre evidence could be questioned as so many other fibres had been found on the bodies. Also, there was the fact that there was some unknown DNA on Anneli Alderton's body, and he asked when it got there. He attacked the fact that areas of Steve Wright's jacket and gloves had not been tested for DNA. He told the jury that the sightings of Steve Wright on CCTV and a number plate recognition camera leaving Ipswich meant that much time had elapsed since the women disappeared on the respective nights, and he wondered what Steve Wright could have been doing for all that time.

Switching the jury's focus to Tom Stephens, Mr Langdale QC referred to Stephens' behaviour during the murder manhunt, including the evidence heard about him threatening to kill an ex-girlfriend after they broke up. He added that Tom Stephens could not provide alibis for the days in question, and reminded the jury of the fact that there was no evidence that Steve Wright knew Tom Stephens.

Timothy Langdale QC repeated that the evidence allowed a reasonable possibility that someone other than Steve Wright, who had nothing to do with him, had committed the murders.

Mr Langdale QC: 'If these points make sense the proper verdict is not guilty.'

That was the end of the defence closing speech, and the court was adjourned for the weekend.

On the morning of Monday, 18 February, Mr Justice Gross began his summing up. He told the jury that it should not be influenced by sympathy for the five victims and their families. Mr Justice Gross: 'The loss of five young ladies is a tragedy. You are likely to have sympathy for the deceased and their families but this must not sway you... You must try this case on the evidence which has been placed before you.'

The judge told members of the jury that they had 'come across a bleak landscape – in simple, brutal terms, the funding of drug abuse by prostitution'. He also added that they should not be influenced by the lifestyles of the five women: 'Whatever drugs they took, whatever the work they did, no one was entitled to do these women any harm.' With reference to Tom Stephens, the first man arrested but not charged, Mr Justice Gross pointed out that Stephens was 'not on trial', but said the defence could not rule out the possibility of his involvement.

Mr Justice Gross reminded the jury that the burden was on the prosecution to prove that Steve Wright was guilty of the murders. He added that the prosecution did not have to prove a motive: 'A case of murder is, and often is, made good without any clear motive.' He also reminded members of the jury that Steve Wright had been indicted on five counts of murder, and that they must consider each count separately. Mr Justice Gross: 'The evidence is different and your verdicts need not be the same.' The judge told the jury that murder was defined as one person unlawfully killing another with the intention to kill or cause grievous bodily harm. He added that there was no question of self-defence in this case.

Mr Justice Gross: 'If you are sure the defendant caused the death of the women, when you are considering them you must be sure that when he pressed their neck he intended to kill her or cause her grievous bodily harm.' Adding that the jury decides intent by considering all that the defendant did and did not do, Mr Justice Gross said: 'Look at his actions before and after the alleged offence. All these things may shed light on his intention at the critical time.' Mr Justice Gross went on to break down the defence and prosecution cases into key points to help give the jury some clarity.

He said that the defence case rested on nine points:

1　Some girls had been to Wright's home address.
2　He knew all five girls.
3　He used the services of four of them.
4　He used prostitutes.
5　Each of the girls had been in his car.
6　The women had taken off their clothes at his house.
7　He drove late at night because of insomnia.
8　He had connections with Nacton and Hintlesham, knew something of Levington but nothing of Copdock (the places where the bodies were found).
9　He had an innocent explanation for the DNA findings.

He said that the prosecution case also rested on nine points:

1 The defendant picked up the women in the order they went missing and at times around their disappearance.
2 Wright had an opportunity to commit the offences because his partner was at work.
3 The CCTV and vehicle number plate recognition evidence.
4 The DNA links between three of the women and the defendant.
5 The fibres linking Wright to all five of the women.
6 The various coincidences suggested by the Crown.
7 The fact that the women started disappearing shortly after Wright began using street prostitutes – and ended after his arrest.
8 The traces of blood found on his clothing from the two women who shed blood.
9 The locations of the deposition sites were familiar to the defendant.

The next day, 19 February, Mr Justice Gross began to sum up each area of evidence in turn, with a focus on the evidence given by Steve Wright himself. When the court was adjourned for the day, it was expected that the jury would retire to consider its verdicts the following day after the judge had finished his summing up.

Indeed, on Wednesday, 20 February, the jury of nine men and three women began its deliberations at 12.05pm after Mr Justice Gross concluded his summing up of the case. Mr Justice Gross asked the jury to seek a unanimous verdict on each count of murder: 'You must reach, if you can, a unanimous verdict. The law allows me in certain circumstances to accept a verdict that is not a verdict of you all. Those circumstances have not arisen.' He went on to say that he would direct them differently at a later stage if necessary.

The jury returned to the court in the middle of the afternoon to ask the judge for clarification of the difference between murder and manslaughter, and then they retired again to deliberate. But there were no verdicts reached that day, and everybody in the court wondered how long it would take to reach them. The tension was mounting almost unbearably as the camera crews were poised outside Ipswich Crown Court.

On the morning of Thursday, 21 February, the jury returned to court to continue its discussions. Steve Wright was of course in the dock, wearing his black suit, white shirt and light blue tie. His father Conrad, seventy-one, and half-brother Keith Wright were watching developments via a video link in another part of the court complex. The families of the victims waited anxiously, hoping that justice would give them some degree of closure. The media, packed in tightly, was holding its collective breath.

In the early afternoon, the jury filed back into Court 1 at Ipswich Crown Court. It had reached verdicts, after eight hours of deliberation. For members of the jury it was the end of almost six weeks of harrowing and complex evidence. For the families of the victims, it was the day they had been waiting for; the moment of truth.

Steve Wright stood in the dock flanked by two security

guards. The jury foreman stood up and read out five verdicts. Each was guilty of murder by a unanimous verdict. As each verdict was read out, there were anguished and relieved cries of 'Yes!' from members of the victims' families. Kim, the mother of Annette Nicholls, broke down in sobs. The mother and sister of Paula Clennell also cried, while the family of Tania Nicol looked immensely relieved. Steve Wright stood emotionless as his future was laid out before him.

Peter Wright QC for the prosecution asked Mr Justice Gross to consider imposing a 'whole life term'. This would mean that Steve Wright would never leave prison.

Outside the court, Detective Chief Superintendent Stewart Gull, who had led the Ipswich police inquiry, told the media: 'These appalling crimes left a community, a county and a nation in profound shock.'

CHAPTER EIGHT

RIPPLES AND AFTERSHOCKS

The guilty verdicts resonated through the media, and there was blanket coverage for the next two days, with every news bulletin and newspaper dominated by the story. Steve Wright's face was everywhere; every aspect of his past and the crimes he committed was examined in detail.

On the night of the guilty verdicts the families of some of the victims gave press conferences, and whilst their relief was plain, they were naturally still full of anger and bitterness at the way that Steve Wright had snatched their loved ones from them. Two of the victims' families called for the return of the death penalty. A police spokesperson acting on behalf of the family of Tania Nicol said: 'These crimes deserve the ultimate penalty.' Meanwhile Craig Bradshaw, the brother-in-law of Paula Clennell, said: 'Justice has been done. I wish we still had the death penalty.' These reactions were understandable in the circumstances, and they initiated a political debate. On the long-running BBC topical debate programme 'Question Time', politicians were asked that very evening whether capital punishment should return.

It should be remembered that Steve Wright had yet to be sentenced. The following day, Friday, 22 February, he returned to Ipswich Crown Court. Arriving from Chelmsford Prison early in the morning, he was led into court at 10.30am. It was known that he would be given five mandatory life sentences, but the judge had yet to set tariffs and this would determine when Steve Wright could apply for parole. However, Mr Justice Gross responded to the call from the prosecutor Peter Wright QC to impose a 'whole life' term. This meant that Steve Wright would die in prison and there was no chance that he would ever be released. Only around thirty-five murderers in Britain were serving 'whole life' terms at this time. They are relatively rare, and up until quite recently only the Home Secretary could impose a 'whole life' term. These terms are intended only for multiple murder and sadistic and callously premeditated murder. Mr Justice Gross had used the newly granted powers. This seemed to set something of a trend: just a few days later a 'whole life' term was handed out to Levi Bellfield for the murder of two young women and the brutal attempted murder of a third.

Steve Wright remained seated during sentencing, as the judge said that he could. He was wearing his dark suit, but had no tie on that day. Wright showed no emotion as he learned that he would never be released. At the end of the proceedings, there was some delay before Steve Wright was taken away from the court in Her Majesty's Prison van No. 24, escorted by three motorcycle outriders and two police cars. Outside the court, in addition to the large media presence, a small crowd of local people had gathered, and as the van pulled away from the court precinct there were some anguished cries of abuse from the crowd. 'Scum!' and 'Bastard!' were easily audible, but whether Wright heard them inside the reinforced van is unclear. He was taken back to Belmarsh Prison in south-east London, to his special cell, where he would undoubtedly remain on suicide watch. It was thought that Wright would be held there only on a temporary basis, to be moved to Wakefield Prison in Yorkshire (where Soham murderer Ian Huntley had served the early years of his sentence) or to Whitemoor Prison in March, Cambridgeshire, the latter being not so very far from Ipswich.

The families of the five murdered women were guided away from the court by police officers. They made no further statements then, but when questioned from a distance, Tania Nicol's aunt turned and shouted to the media that justice had been done. The father of Gemma Adams, Brian, had said the day before: 'I'm so relieved that it's all over.' Meanwhile, Jim Duell, the father of Tania, had reiterated that he had not known that Tania was a prostitute, and that the police could not tell him that she was as she was an adult. He said that he would have tried to stop her if he had known.

Steve Wright's sister was in court for the sentencing; she was in tears. His half-brother Keith Wright told Sky News: 'It all seems surreal. It hasn't sunk in yet... He was always so shy and laid-back, he would back away from everything. All this has come out now – it's not the person I knew.'

The Deputy Chief Constable of Suffolk Constabulary, Jaqui Cheer, who had been so intensely involved in the police inquiry, said: 'These events have been integral to everybody's lives.'

Steve Wright's defence team was considering if there were any grounds for an appeal, although this is entirely routine at the end of a big trial.

That same day it was reported that Tom Stephens, the first man to be arrested in the inquiry, denied any involvement in the killings, and stated that he had no link with Steve Wright. He said: 'During the court case, one side attacked me and the other chose not to challenge what was said about me. I had no opportunity to defend myself.'

The sentencing of Steve Wright brought to an end a nightmare for the town of Ipswich. It had been almost sixteen months since the first woman, Tania Nicol, went missing, and fourteen months almost to the day that Steve Wright had been arrested. While there had been a media blackout during that period for legal reasons, the people of Ipswich had nonetheless lived under the shadow of the terrible events of 2006 for all of that time. The public presence outside the court may have been thin during the trial, but this was no doubt because local people were sure that Steve Wright was the killer and that the police had got the right man.

The period between the charging of Steve Wright on 21 December 2006 and the guilty verdicts that came in on 21 February 2008 was naturally *sub judice* and the media was unable to report anything about him. Now that this barrier was lifted, all sorts of revelations came out about Steve Wright's past.

On the evening of the guilty verdicts, the BBC broadcast a film segment from the early 1980s. It was from their archives and was part of the then popular 'Whicker's World' programme, a travel and culture show fronted by the veteran broadcaster Alan Whicker. In this episode, the cameras follow the crew of the QE2 liner, and in the clip shown, the crew is ashore in Thailand. Incredibly, sitting in a bar is Steve Wright as a young man, probably then in his early twenties. With his back to the camera, and wearing no top, he is having his back caressed by a Thai woman who looks suspiciously like a prostitute. It is definitely Steve Wright, but looking much younger, slimmer and with more hair, which was brown in colour. It was an unsettling image to see, filmed about a quarter of a century earlier.

But that was not all. On the same bulletin that night came the startling revelation that Steve Wright had allegedly married one more time when he was in Thailand, years after the footage was taken. As we saw in Chapter Six, five or six years before his arrest Steve Wright had suddenly sold his possessions and gone off to Thailand. It now transpired that Wright had met a Thai woman there and married her. However, it did not work out, and as reported on BBC News on 21 February, the woman allegedly cheated him out of all of his money. Steve Wright returned to Britain embittered and declared himself bankrupt, it was said. It was also alleged that Wright tried to commit suicide at this time, and that he had tried to end his life on an earlier occasion too.

Steve Wright's father, seventy-one-year-old Conrad, had gone to visit him in Belmarsh Prison when he was awaiting trial, but apparently when Conrad got there his son refused to see him. However, a letter written in prison by Steve Wright to his father was leaked to the media. In one part Steve Wright had written: 'Whenever I get upset, I tend to bury it deep inside – not a healthy thing to do, I suppose.' In another excerpt he wrote: 'I have seen too much anger and violence in my childhood to last anyone a lifetime.'

A journalist was also afforded access to 79 London Road where Wright was arrested. Eerily, in spite of the police searches, it had been left in a very similar state to how it was on the early morning of 19 December 2006. There was even some food left in a frying pan, and there were cuddly toys in the bedroom. There was also a Christmas card that Steve Wright had written to his common-law wife Pamela. It read: 'I love you very much. My life would be empty without you.'

In the *Sun* newspaper on 22 February 2008, the day of Steve Wright's sentencing, there was an interview with Conrad Wright. The headline read 'My Son Should Die For His Evil Crimes', an echo of what two of the victims' families had said. During the interview, it was reported that seventy-one-year-old Conrad had cried.

Conrad said: 'I understand how the families would want the death penalty. If it were my daughter I'd feel the same. What kind of monster is he? He has changed beyond recognition. This person is not the son I knew.' He went on to say that he had disowned his son, and that he would not visit him in prison. Conrad: 'He has been lying all the time. He caused all that stress by claiming to be not guilty. He made the families sit through a trial. When he had problems before he attempted to take his own life. Why didn't he just do it this time?'

It was reported that Steve Wright was 'scarred' when his

mother left when he was nine years old, and he did not see her again for twenty-six years. When his mother got back in contact, Steve had found it difficult to accept her. Conrad: 'He got boozed up. He had a grudge and kept saying, "Why did you leave me? Why did you come back now?"'

Conrad said that Steve had actually made three suicide attempts in his life, usually prompted by a woman leaving him. His half-brother Keith also told the media that Steve Wright was found 'gassed out of his brain' in a car in 1994, and that doctors said it was a miracle he survived. Conrad said that his son 'may have developed a loathing for women'. Conrad went on to recount how his son would store up his anger and then eventually hyperventilate and pass out, and also that Steve was a fan of horror films.

Referring to the murders, Conrad said: 'Something has triggered this. Did the girls taunt him because he couldn't perform?'

Conrad said that he thought that there could have been an accomplice helping his son: 'I don't think he is clever enough to carry this out and not be caught red-handed.'

One of the things that Conrad had found most difficult to come to terms with was the way in which his son had left the bodies naked in the open air. He said that he had since visited all of the murder sites and paid his respects. Conrad: 'What I find hardest to accept is the way the bodies were left. Just dumped, naked, like they are worthless. That was the worst thing of the lot, I think. How could he? This I can't understand. It's a horrible way to treat somebody. My thoughts are with the families and the poor girls that died.'

On the same day, there was an interview in the *Daily Mirror* with Diane Cole, the second wife of Steve Wright.

The headline read 'I Married A Monster'. As we saw in Chapter Six, Diane met Steve on the QE2 and they married in 1987, and took over the running of a pub, the Ferry Boat Inn on the edge of the Norwich red light district. Diane spoke of when they first met: 'Everywhere I went he appeared. I couldn't escape him. He took it that we were a couple, and I just went along with it. He never talked much. But he'd bring me gifts. Gradually I realised that he was taking control of my life.'

Diane went on to talk about the jealous and possessive side to Steve Wright. Talking about their time on the QE2 she said: 'He stopped me going to other crew's cabins. He wanted me to wait alone in my cabin for him. He'd always ask me "Where have you been?" If he found I wasn't in the cabin, he'd wait until I got back and batter me. He'd never say sorry and it was never spoken about.'

She remembered a time when she went ashore in Hawaii with some other crew members: 'When I got back on board he'd written on the cabin door, "Slag, whore, hope Jeff was better than me." In the cabin he told me, "You liked Hawaii that much I thought I'd make you some grass skirts" – he'd cut all my uniform into shreds. Then he went for me with the blade, lunging at me and sticking the knife in the door.'

Incredibly Diane went on to marry Steve Wright. Diane: 'Looking back, I'm so angry with myself for not doing anything. But I was under his control and thought he'd change once we got off the ship. If anything, he got worse.' She went on to talk about the marriage, which they went through with largely to get a pub licence. Diane: 'As soon as we'd made our vows he didn't speak to me. He didn't even dance with me and later on just said, "I suppose we'd better consummate the marriage." After we got our first pub I didn't sleep with him again.'

But his controlling nature and violence did not stop there. On one occasion when she was making the bed when they were staying with Conrad and Steve's stepmother Valerie, Steve flew into a rage. Diane: 'He said, "The sheets aren't straight." I was laughing, thinking it was a joke. Before I knew it, he was banging my head against the wall. I was screaming for help but he just kept on doing it.'

Diane said in the interview that Steve Wright began leaving the pub after closing time each night, locking her in. When she discovered that he was sleeping with two 'mistresses', she publicly announced it at a staff party. That night when she went to bed, she said that Steve came upstairs: 'He dragged me by my feet off the bed, ranting and raving, and said he'd come up every half an hour to get me. He was true to his word. He came up about three times, pulling me off the bed, throwing the furniture around. I barricaded myself in. But he got in and hit me so hard I was knocked out.' They were divorced in 1989.

Also in the *Daily Mirror* that day was an interview with the son of Steve Wright's partner Pamela, Jamie Goodman. He had stayed with them for three weeks in December 2006 when the police manhunt was on – it might be remembered that Jamie's cigarette ends were found in Wright's Ford Mondeo car. Jamie said that one day Pamela had been talking about the murders, and saying how terrible it was. Jamie said that Steve had said to Pamela: 'Get a rape alarm and watch out for yourself.'

Jamie spoke about Wright's character: 'Steve seemed every inch the traditional man. He expected his woman to be chained to the kitchen sink. It really annoyed me. He'd get in and wake up mum to cook his tea (Pamela worked nights). He'd sit watching western films or golf without a word to anyone. She'd go back to bed the minute he had his food. There were no hugs or kisses.' Jamie continued: 'He was meticulous about everything. He refused to put on a shirt without mum pressing it first. We had a few beers together but he never let go. He had to be in control and hardly smiled.'

Jamie said that when he stayed with them, they would all sit in silence: 'I stayed with them for three weeks and we'd sit in silence at the breakfast table every morning. It made me sad for mum.'

Pamela Wright herself was interviewed on Sky News on 25 February. Speaking to the journalist Kay Burley, Pamela said that she no longer recognised the man who made her 'feel like a schoolgirl' when they first met in a bingo hall in 2000. Pamela, sixty, said: 'I really don't know him at all.'

Pamela was asked if their lack of a regular sex life (as previously reported in the media) might have been a contributing factor to Steve Wright's behaviour. With dignity, Pamela said: 'Maybe, but I don't know that now, I don't know if he was doing it when we did have a sex life.'

Pamela also said that Wright had told her that he had known the missing estate agent Suzy Lamplugh: 'I think we were watching either "Crimewatch" or something like that. She came on and he said I used to know her.'

In the *Metro* newspaper on 22 February, there was an interview with a prostitute called Tracy Russell. She said that she had had sex with Steve Wright after his first victim was found (the week of 12–19 December 2006) and that he had behaved differently on that occasion. She said that she had known him for three years and felt safe with him. However, on that night, she felt differently. Tracy Russell: 'He pinned me down. He never used to do that. It did scare me because it wasn't like him. He was a bit nasty. He said to me, "I don't want to rush tonight, I will pay you extra." Then he heard a bang and he said, "Quick, get out!" We didn't have sex and that noise probably saved my life. It must've been Pam. I think it could've been a car door.'

Tracy Russell said that Steve Wright was 'all sweaty' that night. But his car was a different matter: 'His car was immaculate inside that night. It smelt weird, like it had been cleaned. When I heard he had been charged I thought, "Oh my God, I was in his house." I never thought it would be him.'

It is the burning question that everybody wants an answer to: why did Steve Wright do it? There can be no definitive answers, but with the facts that are available, it is possible to venture some informed speculation.

Firstly, there is the issue of Steve Wright's background. His father's career in the RAF and the family's continual relocation during his childhood perhaps set a transient pattern to his life. This is not what makes a serial killer, but in his case may have contributed to an insecure mindset. Then his mother left when he was nine years old. If excerpts from the letter that Steve Wright wrote his father Conrad from prison are considered, a hazy picture emerges: 'I have seen too much anger and violence in my childhood to last anyone a lifetime,' and 'Whenever I get upset, I tend to bury it deep inside.'

What anger and violence did Steve Wright see or experience in his childhood? It seems clear that he felt anger at being left by his mother Patricia, as it would appear that he was still unable to deal with that perceived rejection when she contacted him again twenty-six years later, when he was in his mid-thirties. But this is a relatively common phenomenon. In itself it is unlikely to have been enough to make him into a serial killer. But what else did he see or experience? There are many unanswered questions here.

His early mistrust of women may have become a self-fulfilling prophecy in later life as we see that his relationships with women were largely unsuccessful. Wives and girlfriends left him, no doubt often because of his allegedly unreasonable behaviour towards them. Is it possible that this added to his feelings of abandonment and perceived rejection by his mother, and grew inside him until he exploded with rage?

It certainly seems that Steve Wright was prone to bottling up his anger, appearing quiet and taciturn to those around him. But was he really in control? If the words of his second wife Diane are to be believed, then he was a violent husband, not bottling up his anger at all, but taking it out on her. Yet he does not seem to have ever been violent towards Pamela, his last partner. Had he gradually learned over the years to keep his violence outside the home, to keep the two parts of his life separate?

The idea that Steve Wright lived a double life is a theme that has recurred throughout this story. There was the quiet man, the golfer, the immaculate dresser. Then there is the gambler, the frequenter of prostitutes, the prowler. Many serial murderers have lived in compartments such as this. Dr Harold Shipman was a trusted and respected doctor. John Wayne Gacy, who killed over thirty men and boys in Illinois, USA in the 1970s was a building contractor and a part-time clown at children's parties. Hyde may overtake Jekyll at certain times, but both are always present in a serial killer. If the 'Jekyll' or normal side of Steve Wright had not existed, then no woman would ever have got into his car.

The Yorkshire Ripper Peter Sutcliffe first attacked a prostitute when he was cheated of five pounds by a working girl. He went on to murder thirteen women, and most of them were prostitutes. Could it be that Steve Wright had a rage festering inside him, which built to resentment that he could no longer control? Was his anger directed at women generally, or prostitutes in particular? Or were they just easy and accessible targets?

The leading criminologist Colin Wilson has said that he believes that the Ipswich murders were the end of a cycle, and not the beginning. If this is the case, then the experience with his Thai wife could not have been the trigger. The possibility of other murders will be discussed in the next section.

As we saw in Chapter Four, the Ipswich killer fits the power/control type of serial offender. Steve Wright was undoubtedly an 'organised' offender, planning and executing quite expertly; the way that he continued to kill despite a huge police manhunt must have taken some acumen. Of course, the idea of an accomplice has never been ruled out, nor should it be until there is definite proof otherwise. The prosecution at the trial called the five murders a 'campaign' and surely no better word can be found. A campaign takes strategy, and Steve Wright – perhaps with an accomplice – certainly had one.

The themes of power and control are key here. The very

act of paying for sex might have given him a sense of power and control – the idea of a woman as a commodity. What about the role of fantasy? We can only speculate. He was allegedly violent to at least one woman in everyday life, so what could his fantasies have been like? If Steve Wright felt abandoned and used by women, then killing them must have represented the ultimate control over them.

Then we must consider his modus operandi. The first two women, Tania Nicol and Gemma Adams, were found in water, and this seemed to show a sense of forensic awareness and care to conceal the bodies. However, the last three were found on land, and in relatively exposed locations. Did Steve Wright 'get sloppy' as the prosecution alleged? Or did he subconsciously want to get caught? A third theory could be that Wright grew in confidence to such an extent as he continued to kill and remain free that it became a form of supreme arrogance, the 'You can't catch me' scenario. It is also possible that Steve Wright could not admit to himself what he had done, or at least come to terms with it in a realistic way.

The cruciform pose in which the killer arranged the bodies of Anneli Alderton and Annette Nicholls is also striking. Paula Clennell was not left in this way, but the police were quite certain that she had been left in a hurry; perhaps Wright was disturbed or jumpy in some way. The cruciform shape obviously has religious connotations, and this would have been consistent if the first two women had been left in this way too. A 'visionary' or messianic killer may see killing his victims as a form of salvation with himself as their saviour, particularly if the victims are prostitutes, the 'clean up the streets' credo. Does the fact Tania and Gemma were found in water also have religious overtones, with water as a cleansing agent? But perhaps the answer is far more mundane. As we saw in Chapter Four, after the first two bodies were found there was much media speculation regarding the type of killer involved; one of those put forward was the visionary killer. Could Wright have read this or seen it on television, giving him a bizarre idea? Was he enjoying his mysterious infamy and the fear he was creating? Or was he just trying to mislead the police, making them take the inquiry down the avenue of religious fanaticism?

There may never be concrete answers to these questions. Knowing the identity of the killer is only the beginning. Unless Steve Wright opens up and tells the truth, we will never know for sure why he did it. And even if he did open up for us, could we believe him?

Two approaches were made by the author to Steve Wright's solicitor in an attempt to gain access to him, to hear his side of the story. Both were unsuccessful.

Most serial killers begin to murder in their twenties or early thirties. Steve Wright was forty-eight when he committed the Ipswich murders, so if it really was the 'end of a cycle' as Colin Wilson said, then there could have been earlier killings. The media coverage in the days after Steve Wright was found guilty brought up many questions about other unsolved cases (see Chapters Two and Five). The fact that he had worked in the red light district of Norwich in the late 1980s and allegedly still cruised for prostitutes there as late as the mid-1990s gave much food for thought.

The key cases that were reported were that of twenty-two-year-old Michelle Bettles who worked as a prostitute in Dereham and was found strangled after vanishing from the Norwich red light district in 2002. In 2000, Kellie Pratt, twenty-nine, disappeared from the same area. Her body was never found. A year earlier in 1999, a seventeen-year-old student called Vicky Hall vanished from Trimley St Mary (not the Trimley St Martin where Tom Stephens lived) near Ipswich when she was walking home. Her body was found in Stowmarket, Suffolk. In 1993, twenty-six-year-old Mandy Duncan disappeared from the Ipswich red light district. She was also never found. Finally, there was sixteen-year-old Natalie Pearman, who was last seen in the Norwich red light district, and her body was found outside the city in a local beauty spot. She too had been strangled.

On 22 February 2008 after Steve Wright's sentencing, Deputy Chief Constable Jaqui Cheer gave an interview to the BBC outside Ipswich Crown Court. When asked about these unsolved cases, she said: 'Links to other crimes are speculation at this point.' She went on to explain that all of the Ipswich inquiry information would be stored so that other forces could access it at any time if they wanted to investigate any unsolved cases. However, on the same day the *Daily Telegraph* reported that the police wanted to interview Wright over all of these cases.

But the case that got the most coverage was that of Suzy Lamplugh. Working as an estate agent when she disappeared in south-west London in July 1986, she had gone to show a house to a prospective buyer called 'Mr Kipper'. It was reported widely in the media that Steve Wright had met Miss Lamplugh regularly after they left the QE2, when he ran a pub in Brixton, south London.

Diane Cole, Steve Wright's second wife, also worked on the QE2 at the same time as Wright and Lamplugh. She told the *Daily Telegraph* on 22 February that she had seen Wright talking to Lamplugh, and that she believed he had been flirting with her. Diane Cole also said: 'I'm sure Steve used the word "kipper" as slang for face. He used to say, "What's up with your kipper?"'

The father of Suzy, Paul Lamplugh, seventy-six, said: 'The police dealing with Suzy's disappearance have remained in touch with me over the years and I speak to them every six months or so. They have discussed Steve Wright with me before. The last time they were in touch was just before the trial started. They certainly haven't ruled anything out, and I know they have been in touch with Suffolk Constabulary. Perhaps now the Metropolitan Police will press on with a full investigation into the possibility Steve Wright was responsible for Suzy's disappearance.'

A Scotland Yard spokesman said: 'We are not prepared to discuss who we may or may not interview in connection with an ongoing investigation.' Another source said: 'We would like to speak to him about this, even though we have no direct evidence to link him with Suzy Lamplugh's disappearance.'

On 25 February it was reported in the *Metro* newspaper that former Detective Superintendent Jim Dickie, who had originally led the Suzy Lamplugh inquiry, was convinced that convicted murderer John Cannan (earlier linked to the case) was the man responsible for the abduction and murder of twenty-five-year-old Suzy.

The previous sixteen months had been a whirlwind for the Suffolk Police. It had been the biggest inquiry ever mounted in the county, with help from other police forces, and the total cost was more than twenty million pounds. But the hard work and professionalism they had displayed had been rewarded, and the killer of five women was behind bars, for literally the rest of his life.

That inquiry had taken in a great deal of traditional police work, but in essence it was the DNA match that led them directly to Steve Wright. Other evidence helped gain his conviction, but without that DNA evidence, he may never have come into the spotlight. And if Steve Wright had not stolen that money from a bar a few years before, his DNA would not have been on the database.

In the days following Wright's conviction, there was a growing call from the police to widen and increase the number of DNA samples on the National DNA Database. Britain already has the largest stock of DNA samples in Europe, but several high-profile cases in a few days led to this initiative by the police. Within days of Steve Wright's conviction, largely thanks to DNA, Mark Dixie was convicted for the rape and murder of eighteen-year-old aspiring model Sally-Ann Bowman, and Levi Bellfield was convicted of the murders of two women and the attempted murder of a third. It is understandable that the police wanted to improve their DNA resources.

However, this was not met with agreement from all quarters. Nick Clegg MP, the leader of the Liberal Democratic Party, gave an interview to the BBC on this issue on 22 February. He said: 'The DNA database is not a magic wand to solve everything... Steve Wright was on the database, but managed to go on and kill five women.'

But the police in Suffolk had much to feel content about. It was a period of time that none of the officers involved would ever forget. The sense of community spirit, humanity mixed with professionalism, and good old-fashioned teamwork had together brought a deadly predator to justice. And as Detective Chief Superintendent Stewart Gull told the media: 'I'll never forget 7pm on 17 December 2006 when I got a phone call telling me that there was a DNA match.'

So the killer was caught, and the families now had a small degree of closure. The people of Ipswich had long returned to normal life, confident that the right man had been charged. And there had been no more murders. However, there was another important area that should never be forgotten. These were the twin problems of drugs and prostitution in the Ipswich red light district that allowed the killer to pick and choose his victims.

Chris Mole, MP for Ipswich, told the BBC that in the early days of the investigation local people were very worried about the long-term effect on Ipswich's reputation, but that they were more optimistic now. He went on to praise the police investigation and the teamwork shown with other forces. He also spoke about the 'Somebody's Daughter' charity, which had been set up in tribute and memory of the murdered women. He said that this charity was continuing to help prostitutes.

Jeremy Pembroke, the leader of Suffolk County Council, also spoke about the support being given to drug addicts and prostitutes in Ipswich, for instance, help with medication and social security benefits, and that a twenty-four-hour helpline had been set up for this purpose. He also said that the number of prostitutes working the streets of the Ipswich red light district had fallen very dramatically – from about twenty-five or thirty at one time (estimates vary) to only two occasional sex workers now. He said that the key was to help women directly and that there had also been a crackdown on kerb-crawlers and drug pushers.

Meanwhile, the Reverend Canon Graham Hedger said that he and many others were helping to get prostitutes off the streets. He added that sadly something like the murders had to happen to get all the agencies working together to combat drugs and prostitution. He said: 'Sympathy and compassion are the hallmarks of Ipswich.'

In the words of Brian Tobin, the director of the Iceni Project, a charitable trust set up to help drug users: 'Prior to these murders, very little money was put into this area but we have since managed to engage with street workers, and only two or three work the streets occasionally now.' He added: 'It would have been outrageous if we didn't do something.'

There was also a press conference given by the Project for Street Operation Strategy. This agency had been set up to remove street prostitution from Ipswich. It was said that the murders had given focus and much information about the problem of street prostitution in the town, and that it was about prevention, stopping women from falling into the drug and prostitution trap in the first place. In attempting to do this, 'the support of the community has been imperative'. The intelligence gathered from local men who had been accosted by prostitutes and local women accosted by kerb-crawlers had been vital.

The key was a coordinated approach to the problems. In the case of drugs, the aim was to make sure that treatment services were available to vulnerable women and that they were helped to develop routes out of prostitution. The core issues were housing and benefits, which provided stability to work.

A question was asked about whether the dramatic drop in street prostitution in Ipswich had led to displacement of the women into nearby towns and cities. A spokesperson said that the campaign had links to other cities such as Colchester and Norwich and that information about any displacement was fed back to them so they could deal with it.

It was also revealed that about 130 men had been arrested as a result of the new 'zero tolerance' approach to kerb-crawling.

In another interview for the BBC, a representative of the Prostitutes' Collective had a different view. She said: 'Women still do not feel safe in Ipswich and around the country.' She added that 'Police crackdowns are very dangerous,' and that 'Prostitution should be decriminalised.'

The effect of the murder campaign carried out by Steve Wright, which the Home Office called 'an evil and depraved crime', was large in Ipswich. The community was shaken to its very centre; local people questioned their own surroundings and their own attitudes. Above all, they wondered how it could happen there. But the way that the drug and prostitution problem had been dealt with meant at least that something positive had come from the trauma and chaos. However, it was vital that this should be maintained, as it would be all too easy to slip back into complacency. The scars left by Steve Wright will never disappear, but hopefully they will fade with time.

It was reported in the *News of the World* that Steve Wright had made a phone call to his brother David Wright from prison, which had been taped. It was alleged that Steve Wright had said that he plans to commit suicide.

The words of Steve Wright were allegedly: 'I'm going to do it at the first opportunity I get. Then I want to be cremated and get my ashes scattered at the golf club.'

Perhaps the suicide watch he is under will continue, and he will not get the chance to be at peace like the five young women he killed in acts of cold blooded evil.

As Steve Wright sits in his cell, knowing that he will never see the true light of day again, when he hears the screams through the walls and the flicker of a conscience somewhere inside him, let him remember what he did. Were he to forget for just a moment, if his mind were to block out the misery, every time he picks something up, or touches something, *his hands* will bring what he did back to him.

Tania, Gemma, Anneli, Annette and Paula,

> We live our lives
> In homely hives
> Forgetting ones like you
>
> But your honey hearts
> Will never leave
> As long as we exist
>
> Your memory touches us still

APPENDIX

INTERVIEW WITH DETECTIVE CHIEF SUPERINTENDENT STEWART GULL

The author interviewed the leader of the Ipswich Murders Inquiry at Suffolk Police Headquarters on 19 March 2008. Mr Gull kindly gave the author time from his busy schedule.

Stewart Gull joined Suffolk Constabulary as a cadet twenty-five years ago and has served as both a uniformed and CID officer at every rank. When he led the inquiry, he was the Head of Crime Management. In September 2007 he took up the new role of Head of Protective Services.

It should be remembered just how complex the inquiry that Det. Chief Supt. Gull led was. There were around 300 Suffolk police officers involved, supported by other specialist staff, and a further 300 officers and specialist staff from around forty other police forces from England, Wales and Northern Ireland. There were 176 separate searches carried out, which took 13,000 hours of work by 134 officers from Suffolk and six other forces. The longest fingertip search took twenty-seven officers seven days in terrible weather and the dive team search took fourteen days. There were about 13,000 calls from the public and around 1,570 homes were visited. There were 6,650 statements taken and over 60,000 items of evidence, all of which had to be listed and considered for disclosure to Steve Wright's defence team.

It is also important to stress that Suffolk is one of the safest counties in the UK, with an average of six murders a year. In December 2006, there were six murder inquiries launched in a ten day period in Ipswich alone (the five murders carried out by Steve Wright, plus a fatal nightclub shooting).

NR: Did you think that there was a significant drug/ prostitution problem in Ipswich before Steve Wright's campaign of murder?

SG: Not unlike, no worse than any other provincial town in respect of the availability of drugs. Wherever you look in the UK, however large or small...I guess its proximate location to London perhaps might have an effect. It's a challenge to us, but no more than that. As far as prostitution is concerned, I'm not sure of any date as to when it started, probably back twenty years, that part of Ipswich. We've had varying success at managing that. It's a difficult balance. Quite rightly, local residents take issue with it. But there's always been a hardcore. The tragic events of 2006 bound all the agencies to eradicate prostitution from Ipswich.

NR: Can you tell me something about the feelings of the police as body after body was discovered? It must have been quite a shock...

SG: Shock is an understatement. I think, in our heart of hearts we always feared the worst. We always hoped that perhaps like other working girls who have very chaotic lifestyles, that they would perhaps turn up. I guess we weren't perhaps totally surprised. There had been an awful lot of work gone in before the beginning of December [2006] to try to locate them. So it wasn't totally unexpected. And in some respects we weren't prepared for it. We'd had the nightclub shooting the night before [*Jimoh Plunkett was fatally shot in Zest nightclub in Ipswich on Saturday, 9 December 2006. This is still a live inquiry at the time of writing*]. The force was already under pressure...all sorts of emotions, devastation. You began to think, good grief, what are we dealing with here?

NR: These kinds of cases happen more in the States, and they are quite rare here...

SG: Unprecedented [*due to the speed of events*] – five dead. I described it at the time – it was like responding to a crime in action, with regard to the speed.

NR: The pressure on the police must have been tremendous. Could you tell me how you coped with it?

SG: The pressure was pretty immense. In terms of how we coped, well, it really was a sense of everybody pulling together. In the investigation there was a huge machine in the background, to support the operation.

NR: How complex and demanding were the logistics of the inquiry, and how did you think it went?

SG: It was a challenge. We had the structures in place to

be able to deal with it. There was a team with lots of specialist areas of work going on...inquiry teams, and fielding thousands of calls. So it did bring its pressure. It was demanding, but because we had good people, all of the Constabulary pulled together. Lots of support staff – finding accommodation for people, feeding them. Welfare was a big issue, of course. The overriding challenge was just to deal with the speed with which it was happening. Trying to keep pace with it really.

NR: How significant was the arrest of the first man detained?

SG: As with any inquiry, there are a number of individuals who interest us. As we know, there was one other individual who was raised to suspect status. We'd already planned, before we knew about Steve Wright on Sunday 17 [December 2006], we were going to arrest another suspect on the Monday. There was a second investigation and he remained on police bail while we undertook those enquiries. But there was no evidence found against him.

NR: How confident were you that Steve Wright was the killer on 19 December 2006, the day of his arrest?

SG: I think I've said before that the defining moment was at 7pm on Sunday 17 December. I was in the canteen, grabbing a bite to eat. And one or two of my management team sidled up to me and said, 'Stewart, we've got something'. We got a DNA profile from one of the victims – that's not who I expected them to say. He wasn't on the radar at that stage. He was in the system, we already knew about him. He had been questioned as part of an anniversary road check. It was a defining moment. I made the decision that we weren't going to arrest him immediately. We would benefit from preparation. But he still presented a significant risk, so he was immediately raised to suspect status and put under surveillance.

NR: The DNA evidence: there's been a lot of talk from the police, especially since the Levi Bellfield conviction (for the murder of two women and the attempted murder of a third woman, made largely on the basis of DNA evidence) about whether the National DNA Database should be widened. I wondered what you thought about that, and why?

SG: The Database is a tool for crime investigation. Since its introduction it's been broadened slightly, and we now take DNA not just from those individuals who are charged. I recognise the Human Rights aspect. With regard to broadening it further, the police on a national level welcome that debate. But we need to recognise the limitations it would have. We have a transient population now, haven't we, and people move about – the world is a small place. We need to welcome the debate, and see where that takes us.

NR: Were there any points, during the trial, where the police were concerned that Steve Wright might not be convicted?

SG: He had a good defence team, and rightly so. We were very confident that we had a strong case. There were highs and lows.

NR: How did it feel when Steve Wright was convicted, and then given a Whole Life sentence the next day?

SG: Relief – how I managed to walk from the police room when the jury was coming back, I was racing. I think we always knew that the weight of expectation was pretty immense. There were lots of reasons, for the families, for the community, for over a year. We recognised that the spotlight was on 'UK Policing Plc'. Mixed emotions, relief, and again the following day when the Judge passed sentence.

NR: What was the impact on the community of Ipswich during the murder hunt, and what do you think will be the long-term impact of these terrifying events?

SG: It's a close-knit community, largely rural, but with some large urban centres. The community impact was significant. Whether the fact that they were all working girls made a difference or not, I expect it did to a limited extent. That just added to the pressure. As to the longer-term impact, I guess time will tell. Hopefully Ipswich will recover, and not be known because of a serial killer. It's a very vibrant town, and lots of successful businesses work here. It's a good place to live and work. Hopefully the long-term impact won't be significant. The successful outcome will assist. As I indicated earlier, it has been complex and challenging. Though in the course of time when Ipswich (Town FC) get promoted to the Premiership...We are a safe county. Crime is low. In this last year, crime across the piste is down by 5%.

***

On the very day that this interview took place, it was announced that Steve Wright was seeking permission to launch an Appeal against his conviction.